D1444234

It's Fun To Be Your
Sister

BECKY FREEMAN JOHNSON

HARVEST HOUSE PUBLISHERS

EUGENE, OREGON

Unless otherwise indicated, all Scripture quotations are taken from the New King James Version. Copyright ©1982 by Thomas Nelson, Inc. Used by permission. All rights reserved.

Verses marked NIV are taken from the HOLY BIBLE, NEW INTERNATIONAL VERSION®. NIV®. Copyright ©1973, 1978, 1984 by the International Bible Society. Used by permission of Zondervan. All rights reserved.

Verses marked KJV are taken from the King James Version of the Bible.

Becky Freeman Johnson: Published in association with the literary agency of WordServe Literary Group, Ltd., 10152 S. Knoll Circle, Highlands Ranch, CO 80130.

Every effort has been made to give proper credit for all stories, poems, and quotations. If for any reason proper credit has not been given, please notify the author or publisher and proper notation will be given on future printing.

Cover by Jeff Franke Design and Illustration, Minneapolis, Minnesota

Cover photo © LM Productions / Digital Vision / Getty Images

IT'S FUN TO BE YOUR SISTER
Copyright © 2007 by Becky Freeman Johnson
Published by Harvest House Publishers
Eugene, Oregon 97402
www.harvesthousepublishers.com

Library of Congress Cataloging-in-Publication Data
Johnson, Becky Freeman, 1959-
It's fun to be your sister / Becky Freeman Johnson.
    p. cm.
ISBN-13: 978-0-7369-1804-6
ISBN-10: 0-7369-1804-3
1. Mothers—Religious life. I. Title.
BV4529.18.J632 2007
242'.6431—dc22
                                                            2006016227

Printed in China

07 08 09 10 11 12 13 / RDS-CF / 10 9 8 7 6 5 4 3 2 1

○ ○ ○

To my sister,
Rachel Ann St. John-Gilbert,
whose fun-loving nature is only slightly eclipsed
by the ridiculous length of her name.

Rachel,
You've entertained me for years
on long car trips, at kitchen tables, and
in quaint coffee shops.
What a joy to watch you grow up to be
a gifted and hilarious writer standing tall
in your own literary spotlight.
This one's for you!

○ ○ ○

Acknowledgments

With deepest love and fond affection to my witty sister, Rachel. I tease about her methodically slow nature in the book you are about to read. Ironically, at this writing she's on the way to see me from the Denver airport. Her plane, coming in from Texas, landed at 11:30 AM. It was 2:00 PM when she finally decided to get her rental car and leave the airport. Why? Besides the fact that she has two little girls in tow, she's been enjoying the airport ambiance—the shops, the bathrooms, the eateries, the people. She stops and smells more roses in a single afternoon than most people do in a lifetime. You've got to love a sister like this! (And thank her for all the material she gives to your writing life.)

Also, a warm hug of gratitude to my adopted sister, Lindsey O'Connor. I lunched with her yesterday, chatted on the phone with her today, emailed in between. If that doesn't qualify us for sisterhood, what does? (If in doubt, read on!) Not only is Lindsey as close as kin in the daily soap opera/sitcom affairs of life and family, she's a spiritual and professional encourager. Thank you, Linds!

My heartfelt gratitude to the folks at Harvest House Publishers, particularly Bob Hawkins Jr., Terry Glaspey, Carolyn McCready, and LaRae Weikert for not just talking about grace but for actually being "God's love with skin on" to me when my life, as I knew it, blew into so many pain-filled pieces. Thank you from the depths of my soul for reminding me of who I am and trusting me to continue sharing my heart through the written word. Thanks to the ever-encouraging and talented Jean Christen and Barbara Gordon for doing the fine-tuning of this manuscript. These gals deserve some sort of special award from above for working with this particularly scatterbrained author.

Last, but certainly not least, I want to thank the love of my life, my husband, Greg Johnson, for putting me back together again—for loving me truly, deeply, madly every blessed day of my life. Your kind and tender husbanding has created the garden from which I've been able to blossom into an ecstatically happy wife, serene mother, and creative writer.

Oh, and you just happen to be the world's best literary agent.

I love you so.

Contents

1

Uncommon Ground

If we both think exactly alike,
one of us isn't needed.
ANONYMOUS

There are three kinds of people in this world: right brain creative types, left brain organizers, and people who cannot seem to locate cerebral matter in either hemisphere. I am whichever brain it is that can organize her thoughts on paper, be a member of a number of honor societies, and still manage to wear her dress inside out all day without noticing it.

People seem to be born either basically organized or artistically creative, but rarely both. My little sister, Rachel, and I are prime examples of both extremes.

When we were children living at home, her belongings were so organized I could not filch so much as one M&M from a mammoth Easter basket without being called to account for it.

I recall a morning when I desperately needed to borrow a clean blouse from her closet because mine were all in use—piled on the carpet in the corner of my room to hide from my mother a Kool-Aid stain. I opened Rachel's door ever so quietly and tried to tippy-toe into her room without waking her. She never moved, never opened an eye, but said in what I thought was an unnecessarily threatening voice, "Don't even think about it."

Even our choice in clothes reflected our different personalities. As we grew to be teenagers, Rachel opted for a few well-tailored quality suits. I, on the other hand, had a closet full of bargains with lots of ruffles, lace, and color.

Our courtships and subsequent marriages also revealed our right brain/left brain contrasts. I fell hopelessly in love at the ripe old age of 15 while digging ditches for an orphanage on a mission trip to El Salvador. My beau and I married at 18 and 17, respectively, thinking very little about the things money could buy—food, clothing, shelter, gasoline. We'd simply live on our love, which at that naïve time (having more hormones than brains) seemed completely enough.

But my little sister kept her head about her, even in matters of courtship. First, she graduated from college and then, at a respectable age, met her potential lifetime partner, Scott—Scott St. John-Gilbert III, no less. (I like to call him Gilley.) Before rushing into marriage, Rachel and Gilley ran through a series of personality compatibility tests and endured agonizing spiritual searches to determine God's will in the matter. After their tentative budget was planned and their 5-, 10-, and 15-year goals carefully drawn up, they plunged down the aisle with reckless abandon.

With their Five-Year Plan right on track, my penny-wise sister and brother-in-law saved their D.I.N.K (Double Income

No Kids) earnings to purchase a lovely condo overlooking a golf course. On the other hand, after 13 years of marriage, my husband and I bought an 864-square-foot cabin on a lake in the country, then bravely (or crazily) moved in with our four kids. Rachel and Gilley soon purchased a houseful of Ethan Allen furniture, in varying shades of white. When I finally scraped enough pennies together to purchase our first piece of brand-new (not hand-me-down or garage-sale!) furniture, I chose a tan and burgundy print for its ability to blend with peanut butter and jelly.

Little did either of us know that a couple of decades from this period, each of us would face changes so enormous that we'd wonder, at times, if we'd exchanged lives. (Stay tuned.)

In reality, it is the differences between my sister and me that keep us fascinated with each other's lives. We have grown to admire and love each other more with each passing year, due to a good deal of acceptance and understanding, coupled with unconditional love that seems to know no bounds.

Ultimately, love is the only "common ground" two uniquely different sisters ever really need.

○ ○ ○

The body is a unit, though it is made up of
many parts; and though all its parts are many,
they form one body. So it is with Christ.

1 CORINTHIANS 12:12 NIV

2

Birthin' Babies

If you want to know what it feels like to have a baby, Honey, take hold of your upper lip. Now, stretch it over your head.

AUTHOR UNKNOWN

One might expect that in bearing children, we are all sisters under the skin, which is true. However, no two births are ever exactly alike, and Rach and I even bore children under incredibly different circumstances. When my first child, Zachary, was born in the late seventies, the watchword of the young and idealistic was "Back to Nature!" Lamaze was the only way to go. Therefore, I would give birth in the warmth and intimacy of our own home, in natural, cozy, unmedicated, excruciating pain.

My first baby was born after a 28-hour labor, three hours of pushing, and delivered by a male ex-marine sergeant-turned-midwife. One thing about having a marine for a labor coach is that when he barked "Push!"—no matter how exhausted I was, I wasn't about to ignore orders. After two hours of pushing, I would have cheerfully strangled every natural childbirth expert who had ever told me that labor was not really painful, just hard work. Look, I know hard work. I was a friend of hard work. And this was no hard work. This was PAIN. But the nine pound, two ounce miracle that finally made his arrival, was worth it all.

My second child arrived in June, and was oh so much easier. Our garden had yielded its abundance at the same time Ezekiel was born, and my mom still laughs at the memory of bathing her newborn grandson in the kitchen sink alongside five bushels of zucchini, organic, of course. While I was Earth Mother personified, Zeke was the original Cabbage Patch kid.

Baby Number Three, however, would have none of making her appearance on a warm summer morning. Rachel Praise made her debut three days after Christmas in 1982, one of the coldest winters in the history of Texas. My parents and my sister, Rachel, 18 at the time, were visiting for the holidays, and they all needed to return home. I was overdue and felt like a watched pot waiting to boil. Finally, at about two in the morning on December 28, I woke my husband to tell him I was in labor.

"Go back to sleep," my young husband, Scott, yawned. "I don't even think you're pregnant anymore."

The interesting thing is, I managed to do it, but when I next woke up there was absolutely no doubt. The baby's head had crowned. I was pregnant, but I wouldn't be for long.

The scene that followed was like a choppy Keystone Cops episode. I yelled orders while Scott scoured the closet for what would now be our "do it yourself birth kit" since the midwife was 30 minutes away in good weather.

Daddy got on the phone to the midwife, relayed messages to Mother, who hollered them to Scott, who attended to me. In the meantime, Rachel took careful notes in the section of her loose-leaf organizer entitled "Things I Must Never Do." Then she dived in like a trooper, ready to boil rags or tear up sheets.

When our daughter arrived, we named her Rachel, after one of my favorite people in the whole world: my sister.

On the first day of February 1992, my sister gave birth to her first child—her way. She went into labor after a full night's rest, at about seven in the morning, on her day off. Seven-and-a-half hours later, she called me from the exquisitely beautiful and home-like birthing room at the hospital to tell me in graphic detail of the two painful contractions she had endured before calling for the epidural.

"After that, "she reported enthusiastically, "it was great. We all sat around and laughed and played gin rummy." That evening when I called to check on her and her new son, she could hardly talk because she was chewing steak from the candlelight dinner the hospital had served her and Gilley. She apologized for cutting me short, but she had to call the gym and make her next racquetball appointment before it closed.

Good grief! I mentally ground my teeth. *She has managed yuppie childbirth!*

As memories of my totally natural Lamaze, Laboyer, LaLudicrous births swept over me, all I could think was, *What was I thinking?*

In retrospect, I draw some comfort in wondering if the modern way of giving birth in those beautiful birthing rooms with loved ones about would have ever happened if a generation of Mother Earth devotees had not put their collective Birkenstocks down. Maybe I had a tiny part in helping my sister's childbirth experience be one she will always cherish. I hope so. But I'll tell you one thing for SURE. If I ever have another baby (heaven forbid, since I'm nearing the big 5-0!)—I will be the woman shouting "Give me all the drugs you've got!"

Then I'm going to sit back, relax, and watch the painless proceedings as I phone my sister and ask her to bring me the juiciest steak dinner she can find.

○ ○ ○

There shall be no more pain, for the
former things have passed away.

REVELATION 21:4

3

Steel Magnolia Sister

When the mind says, "It's possible!" the body and spirit unite in a supreme effort to prove it.

MY AUNT ETTA LYNCH

Because my Aunt Etta is a woman of near mythic proportions in my family tree, I asked my mother, Ruthie Arnold, to share her own memories of her big sister. The following is Mother's vivid response.

○ ○ ○

The earliest memory I have of my big sister was the day she came home and threw open the front screen and stomped through the door with a flourish.

There she stood, her lovely brunette head erect and defiant under a broad-brimmed white hat, her statuesque figure draped in a white jersey dress. The year was 1941. She was 16 and I was

4, but even at 4, I knew we were about to have a scene. Nobody in our house ever walked defiantly except our daddy. Mostly we walked diffidently.

But Etta was definitely walking defiantly toward my father's bedroom even as I noticed a young man in a sailor's uniform coming up the porch steps just in time to catch the screen door intended to slam behind my sister. I must have followed Etta into the bedroom because I remember the scene quite clearly.

Our father had been lying down (it was midmorning as I recall), and he sat up on the side of the bed. Maybe he had seen the young sailor waiting in the doorway behind her, but he stayed seated, looking at my sister with narrowed eyes. To me she seemed to tower over us all, a figure intent with purpose. Hands on her hips, head thrown back under the white hat, she made her statement.

"I told you if you ever whipped me again I'd be married in two weeks. This is my husband. We were married this morning."

Daddy did not move from his seat on the bed, his elbows resting on his knees, his hands dropped between them. He said words to the effect, "Well, Sis, you've done it now," but rather more pungently than that.

If he said anything else, I don't remember, but that must have been the end of the scene because I seem to remember that she introduced her sailor to the rest of the family, and I think she helped fix lunch, which we all ate together. I don't recall how many of the four younger brothers gathered round the table, big-eyed at such goings-on. Daddy had always been the one in charge, but today, we all knew, Etta was in charge.

She had made her break. Daddy wouldn't ever control her again. Ever. And he would never whip her again either.

She must have changed out of her white jersey dress after lunch because another scene took place that I do not remember, but it has been repeated at every family gathering since 1941. For some reason that afternoon, my brother James was teasing Etta, and she gave chase, her long legs matching him stride for stride until he must have felt her hot breath on his neck. Deliverance came (he thought) when he leaped over a fence and, in a supreme act of recklessness, turned to stick his tongue out at Etta, of all people.

Before he could say, "Nya, nya, you can't catch me," she was over the fence and landed right in his middle, married woman or not.

From that day forward, I knew that if ever there was a member of our family I'd want on my team, it would be my big sister. She crossed a threshold that day, declaring to the world as best as a young girl of 16 could (growing up with few choices and even less money), that she would not be beaten: not by her alcoholic raging father, not even by her good-natured but often-aggravating brothers, and certainly not by the hardships of life.

I know beyond a shadow of a doubt that she helped me get back to my feet in a few dark times as an adult when I felt I couldn't get up again. At those times I heard the echo of her determined voice.

"The Jones' girls may get knocked down, but we always, always, get back up again." At those times, I knew I sure wasn't going to let myself be the first Jones woman to stay flat on her face. How could I face my big sister?

He gives power to the weak, and to those who have no might He increases strength. Even the

youths shall faint and be weary, and the young men shall utterly fall, but those who wait on the LORD shall renew their strength; they shall mount up with wings like eagles, they shall run and not be weary, they shall walk and not faint.

ISAIAH 40:29-31

4

A Sister's Time to Shine

Having been given an introduction to my feisty Aunt Etta in the previous chapter, I'm assuming you may be as curious to hear "the rest of the story" as I was. I wrote my mother Ruthie an email and said, "Don't leave me hanging! Tell me what happened once Etta left the house with her sailor husband as a bride of 16!" One thing you may have realized, if you've read any of my books: The females in my family tree tend not to be boring. Sure we may have our share of normal dysfunctions, but on my mother's side of the family there's an unspoken agreement that at least we will have the decency to make them sound entertaining.

Settle in on the edge of your seat, and I'll allow Mother to continue the tale of her Big Sister Etta.

○ ○ ○

My big brothers, now in their sixties and seventies, still laugh over Etta's statement, at about age eight, that she planned to spend a good deal of her time as an adult lying about on "shif'on" pillows and eating bonbons.

In high school Etta made the National Honor Society at the same time she scrubbed houses for the well-to-do in our small town, walking into town to school, and then on to her work. At the end of the day, she made her way back down the country roads to our house to do what she could to help Mother with her workload. And the money she earned mostly went into Mother's apron pocket to help support our family.

But those days were over now. She had graduated early and with honors, and she had found someone to take her away from her father's heavy hand and the relentless poverty and labor and whippings.

But there was at least one thing Daddy was right about. Sis had really "done it now." The best that could be said about her marriage was that she had jumped from the fire into the frying pan, and a few short years later, she came back to our house (now in town but not much improved) as a single mother, bringing her three-year-old son and four-year-old daughter.

Typical of Etta, she had laid her plans carefully, going through beauty school so that she would be able to support her children before leaving a marriage that had become impossible for her. And by this time, Daddy was barely functional and drinking heavily. I and two older brothers still needed to get through grade school, junior high, and high school, so Etta opened her beauty shop in downtown Sweetwater to put bread on the table for us all.

Yes, Daddy worked occasionally, but mostly he was more problem than problem solver. We three younger ones also worked as we went through school, earning our own spending money.

Mother took care of Etta's children while Etta worked. But how many times I remember when my brothers or I needed to make a choir or band trip or to buy a uniform and there was simply no money in Mother's apron pocket. Etta produced it without complaining, even while she produced grocery money at the end of the week to feed all eight of us, and money to keep the lights on and the house warm.

And then one day a handsome fellow named Jimmy Lynch parked a brand-new Buick by our curb, strolled up the walk to our house, doffing his Stetson hat as he came to call on my big sister. Jimmy had wanted to court Etta when she was 14 and he 21 but Daddy would have none of it.

Now he was back, still single after all these years, and he wanted to court my sister. After her first disastrous marriage, she was gun-shy, as we say in Texas. So Jimmy had to be especially persistent. She had married in haste once and repented at leisure. It took Jimmy a long time to convince her that their marriage would be different.

My brother Lloyd had graduated, Gene was almost there, and I was a junior in high school. Etta figured we could make it without her now. Her own children were preteen, so she packed them up with her and Jimmy and moved to Lubbock where she opened her beauty shop and finished raising her own children. And once again she made her plans. She wanted to learn how to write professionally. It was her dream, and now she wanted to follow it.

So she took courses, and studied, and wrote and wrote, prolifically producing and eventually selling her work.

When Jimmy fell seriously ill with cancer, I sensed a change in Etta. Prayer became like breathing to her, and a prayer chain with friends grew to be a vital part of her life. Faith in God permeated her own natural strength and courage, and with it came deep peace and utter confidence in God…and because of God, confidence in her own ability. Miraculously, Jimmy recovered completely from recurrences of cancer three different times, from a cancer that appeared in three different places. Even the doctors were stunned.

From this experience, along with stories of other answers to prayer, Etta published her first book with Revell: *Help Is Only a Prayer Away.* What a day it was to walk into the small town library in Sweetwater, Texas, and watch my sister, resplendently beautiful, signing copy after copy of her first book.

Many years and many books later, at age 75, and newly widowed, Etta made a declaration to all of us who spent so much time over the years watching her with our mouths wide open. She said, "It's about time I got my journalism degree. I'm going to college."

○ ○ ○

Becky's postscript: Aunt Etta called me at age 80, having just completed the final course required for her graduation: college algebra. Can you imagine tackling algebra at age 80? She had to hire a tutor, but she passed the course.

Can you imagine how hard Etta makes it for the rest of us females in the family tree to complain about *our* little challenges? When I was going through the worst period in my life, in my early forties, watching my marriage of 27 years unravel before my stunned eyes, I have to admit, I was sorely tempted to sit around in bouts of paralyzing self-pity. One day as I was walking around the square in my mom and dad's charming hometown in Texas, I saw a T-shirt that said, "Put your big girl panties on and deal with it!" I thought to myself, *Now that's something Aunt Etta would say. If she made it through, I can make it too!*

If you are going through a tough time, try looking to the sisterhood swinging from the branches of your family tree. Then ask your "survival sisters"—the ones who will help you carry on—to pass down their best big girl panty advice and, whatever challenge you are facing, you'll find the courage to deal with it!

Strength and honor are her clothing;
she shall rejoice in time to come.
She opens her mouth with wisdom, and
on her tongue is the law of kindness.
She watches over the ways of her household,
and does not eat the bread of idleness.

PROVERBS 31:25-27

5

Can I Have This Dance?

*We did a lot of dancing at our house,
fast dancing; everyone in the family was
a dancing fool. I always came down
from my room to dance. When the
music was going, who could resist?*

ANNIE DILLARD

My mother and father have, perhaps, the most lasting and romantic relationship of any couple I've ever known. I think I am only now realizing, and oh so sadly, how few people ever observe such a marriage, much less enjoy one. Mother and Daddy can turn any normal event into a chance for touching and tenderness. Even something as mundane as watching TV means they will soon be getting out a bottle of lotion and giving one another foot massages, a tradition with them. They haven't let up on the romance in the five decades that my sister, brother, and I have been around. Just before we celebrated their fiftieth wedding anniversary this past Christmas in an informal family gathering at my home, my dad asked if he could talk with me a minute.

"If you don't mind, Becky, I'd like to sing a song to your mother."

I thought it was a great idea.

At the anniversary celebration, Dad's baritone voice was as strong as it's always been, and he surprised Mother by gazing into her eyes and singing a tender love song by the country music group Alabama. "Forever's as Far as I'll Go" is a beautiful song that says even when there is gray in our hair, our tender love will go on.

Dad sang beautifully, flawlessly through the end of the song…until he got to the last line. Then he lost it, and Mother stood to let him enfold her in his embrace. Try as he might, he was too choked up with gratitude to finish the last line, the song's title phrase: "Forever's as far as I'll go." There was no need for any words in this moment. Fifty years of wedded bliss, mingled with tears of gratitude, told its story on their faces.

Needless to say, not only were Mom and Dad tearing up, there wasn't a dry eye in the room. (And my eyes are moist again with this retelling.)

Then we all went around the room sharing what we remembered and admired most about their marriage. My sister, Rachel, brought some comic relief when she stumbled and stammered for the right words to express her heartfelt love and gratitude for our parents when finally she blurted, "What I'm really trying to say is: You guys *complete* me!"

We must assume from the moon-eyed looks from their wedding photographs that they were pretty much gone on each other even before my brother, sister, and I were born. Still I know it is a rare and precious treasure to have parents who still have "the look of love" in their seventies that they once shared as twenty-somethings on their wedding day.

What's their secret? They are soulmates and playmates, lovers and laughers. They pray together, and they are good and kind and sweet to each other. But they will tell you in a heartbeat that one of the secrets to their lifelong romance is that it takes two to tango. It takes two people willing to give all they've got to make a marriage great. And then, literally, you must be willing to learn to tango. My parents are dancing fools. Daddy teaches Sunday school at the conservative Baptist church in their small town and even this hasn't deterred them from the dance floor. (In fact, they sneak off with a passel of their Baptist buddies to two-step and Cotton-Eyed Joe as often as they can.) Currently they are taking advanced lessons from a gentleman in his mid-eighties, who they swear is still poetry in motion and as crazy about his wife—who gracefully accompanies him on the dance floor—as my folks are about each other.

A few years ago my mother sent me this note, and gave credit for their joy of tripping-the-light-fantastic, where she felt the credit was due.

> Dear Becky,
>
> Tonight I waltzed with your daddy. It wasn't just any waltz either. We swirled and dipped and side-stepped and swayed, lost in the wonder of the music and each other. And then a thought shafted into my mind with amazing clarity. My sister gave

me this beautiful moment. Etta and Jimmy taught
us to waltz.

Indeed, Etta and Jimmy taught our whole family to dance. I especially think of one memorable, uproarious night, the night we had a hoedown in my parents' living room. I can almost see the furniture pushed back against the wall and hear the country harmonies beckoning us to move our feet in rhythm. Talk about pure, unadulterated fun! All evening long Aunt Etta and Uncle Jimmy—the "Fred and Ginger" of the family room—taught my parents and my siblings and me to schottische, two-step, polka, waltz, and do a line dance to an old tune called "Pinto Beans."

So stunning were Etta and Jimmy when they stepped on a dance floor that folks couldn't help pausing with wistful wonder, backing up as the elegant couple waltzed by, dipping and turning with grace. They moved fluidly, effortlessly, like a pair of swans over a lake of glass.

For a long time I barely listened to anything resembling dance music—especially country music—because after the devastating loss of my nearly three-decades long marriage I was painfully aware that I was no longer a part of a pair. I was trying awkwardly to shuffle-step-hop my way through life without a partner.

Then, just when I thought the music had stopped forever, the kindest man in the world, with a heart overflowing with love, waltzed into my life and into my arms. Turns out Greg Johnson is also a dyed-in-the-wool Rat Pack fan, and soon we were suckers for any love song by Frankie or Deano or Sammy. All of the songs seemed written just for us! Suddenly we were 18 again, humming "You Make Me Feel So Young" and "Young at Heart" between taking anti-aging vitamins and upping our prescriptions for reading glasses.

Our wedding banquet opened with "That's Amoré," followed by the toe-tapping "Dance with Me," and then continued with three hours of music, song, and celebration. My mom and dad gleefully tripped the light fantastic, and my sister hardly paused to take breath between cuttin' the rug.

Ah…if we wait long enough, life really does come back, and often in better ways than we could ever have dreamed.

This week we celebrated the birthday of my eldest son's girlfriend. All three of my sons, who've recently moved to Colorado near Greg and I, will be there. Where? At The Trail Dust, a restaurant that serves up Texas style barbecue ribs with a live, toe-stompin' band on the side. I not only danced a slow dance or two with Greg, but each of my sons also took their turn on the dance floor with their gals. (Especially cute was Zeke with his wife, Amy, now seven months pregnant!) I smiled, remembering how'd I'd passed down Aunt Etta's lessons, teaching my kids how to dance in their stocking feet on the wood dining room floor, all the furniture moved back against the wall. Gabe, our family's Elvis-look-alike, was my only son without a girlfriend at the birthday bash, but that didn't deter him. He couldn't seem to get enough of twirling and two-stepping with me. Though my ol' calves and hips ached, my heart was waltzing on air.

"You're such a good son to dance with a middle-aged lady," I said as I caught my breath during the band's five minute break.

"I love dancing with my mama!" he responded with sincere enthusiasm.

In that moment I echoed my mother's sentiments as gratitude

rose in my heart for her sister, my aunt, for teaching us all how to glide gracefully to the music of our lives.

As Lee Ann Womack sang, "When you get the choice to sit it out or dance"—with your beloved soulmate, or your kids, or a middle-aged mama—"I hope you dance."

○ ○ ○

*When he came near the house, he
heard music and dancing.*

Luke 15:25 NIV

6

An Eye for Detail

"I come in the little things," saith the Lord.
EVELYN UNDERHILL

My sister, Rachel, is not only organized by nature, she is the ultimate connoisseur of life's little things. What's amazing about this is that she is married to a man who pays equal attention to detail. A few years ago when Rach and I arrived at our favorite B&B in Tennessee for our annual sister getaway, she could hardly wait to deliver the detailed room report to her husband, Gilley.

As I plopped my tired body across the bed, I couldn't help overhearing Rachel's side of the telephone conversation. "Hi, Honey, we're here at the Rose Garden! Yes...uh-uh. Jim and Shirley, the B&B owners, were dressed in matching black-and-white striped aprons and chef hats when we arrived. Jim had just made a New Orleans bread pudding—hot out of the oven with a warm vanilla hard sauce. Yeah, and they also arranged a delicate bouquet of tea roses in a tiny antique vase for our bedside tables. And this year they've added a white cotton duvet to the bed linens. Oh, what color are the roses? Hmmm…let's see…one is fuchsia with a hint of ecru, another is a delicate peach—no, wait, I think it may have more of an early spring apricot tint around the outermost petals…"

Oh, brother, I thought. *We could be as old as the Delaney sisters by the time she finishes having her say.*

I opted for a relaxing soak in the hot tub while Rachel and her husband regaled each other with the nuances of the upholstery print on the sofa. Thirty minutes later I strolled in from the hot tub—rested, relaxed, and ready for dinner. To my amazement, Rachel was still doing room detail by phone. To my even greater amazement, Gilley was apparently egging her on, asking question after question, a rapt audience of one.

"The soap is a clear pink glycerin," Rachel was saying, "flat and round, about the size of a diminutive hockey puck. It fits *perfectly* inside the sea-foam green handcrafted pottery dish. I know, I know. It's *unbelievable.*"

My eye-for-details sister should have been one of those hostesses for the Home Shopping Network—the ones with the amazing ability to talk about a pair of colorless polyester pants in the same sparkling detail as one might describe England's crown jewels. Or better yet, she could write those incredible wine descriptions for upperclass menus—the ones that make fine vintages sound so marvelous, they read like personal ads: Rich, full-bodied Burgundy with a come-hither hint of playfulness seeks fruity, crisp Chardonnay with subtle, woodsy overtones.

By the time I'd showered, shaved my legs, dressed, and put on my face, Rachel had finally said so long, farewell, auf Wiedersehen, and goodbye to her hubby. I grabbed the receiver (it was still warm from the heat of over-conversing) and dialed home.

"Hi, there!" I singsonged to the first person who answered the phone. "Aunt Rachel and I are here! Doing great. You guys all right? Okay, then, see ya in a couple of days. Love you too!"

Click.

Done.

"You didn't even tell them about the Pecan Coconut Bohemian Bundt Cake Shirley baked for us!" Rachel exclaimed.

"Trust me," I said, "it's a detail my family can live without." Rubbing my grumbling tummy, I added, "I'm starving. Why don't you go lather yourself up with the rose-scented hockey puck and put on your brown suit…"

"Sienna."

"Come again?"

"It's burnt sienna, with a sepia-toned belt."

I looked toward the ceiling and sighed while my sister flashed a mischievous grin and darted for the bathroom (or should I say, "She ambulated toward the comfort closet adorned in a stunning array of floral linens, delicately accented with a roving vine motif…").

Though I tease Rachel about her eye for detail, it is this notice-the-minutiae trait that prompts her to send birthday cards with funny, personal messages to each of my four children—on their actual birthdays. (All my nieces and nephews know their Aunt Becky just tries to hit the general target month.) When I wrote my first book, it was Rachel's penchant for noticing and commenting on specific passages that encouraged me more than any other. (Who among us, when receiving compliments, doesn't want details, details, and more details?) Then there's the pure fun of having someone along who is so easily amused and excited by life's simple pleasures that most overlook.

People like my sister "squeeze the goody" out of life so that even a simple, well-brewed cup of coffee can be cause for comment and gratitude. They teach us all to pause, stop, breathe in the pleasant aroma of small blessings, and thoroughly celebrate the moments of our lives. In vivid detail.

○ ○ ○

Every good gift and every perfect
gift is from above, and comes down
from the Father of lights...

JAMES 1:17

7

Confused Us Say, "Fortunate Is Girl with Funny Sister"

*We can't all be heroes because somebody
has to sit on the curb and clap as they go by.*
WILL ROGERS

One spring I had several speaking engagements within easy driving distance to Rachel's then Southern-based home of Atlanta. She'd drive to the airport, park her car, and hop into the rental car with me once my plane arrived at the airport. Off we'd go like Ethel and Lucy on a road trip together. On every getaway trip, my notable sister gave me pause to think and often laugh aloud. Perhaps the most amusing thing about Rachel's detail-oriented mind is that she's like having a female Jerry Seinfeld as a sidekick. She's a master at observing the quirks of life and delivers a running commentary with perfect timing and a sharp wit. And it's one of the things I've loved about having my little sister tag along ever since we were kids. When I was dating and she was 11 or 12 (I was five years her senior), she'd often pop up between my boyfriend and me, put her arms around our necks and say, "Just us three again. Where are you two going to take me now?" How could we resist her dimples and dancing black eyes and eager-for-adventure smile?

One week several years ago Rachel and I drove up together to spend the day at a retreat in North Carolina, set on picturesque Lake Lure and surrounded by the blue-green barrier of the Smoky Mountains. The 1930s lodge was picture-perfect, the grounds surrounding it a living bouquet of spring flowers and foliage. (Of course Rachel had researched and found this little haven for us ahead of time.) As we went out to take a morning stroll, we happened upon a pair of cement Chinese dragons placed as exotic accents to the gardens. But as we got a little closer to the Chinese figurines, Rachel's sharp eye—and sharp wit—caught me off guard.

"Hey, Beck—look at those dragons! They're buck-toothed. Those two could eat bamboo shoots through a picket fence."

Sure enough, upon closer inspection I could see that the dragons each sported an amazing set of Billy Bob uppers. Though I am sure the designer meant them to look ferocious, they looked more like dragon twins who just barely graduated from slow class. Each dragon had about 20 teeth, all the same size, like a row of white Chiclets so big they concealed any evidence of a bottom lip.

I couldn't help laughing. "You know, Rach, you're right. I think that's one of the most impressive overbites I've ever seen on a yard ornament."

At this point, Rachel employed her best hillbilly accent, stuck her front teeth out, and took on the persona of the slant-eyed, toothy twin statues. "Why, howdy there, y'all. We're the Bubba

Dragons! Come on in and put yer feet up! How 'bout some moo goo gai pan 'n' grits?"

By this time I was laughing so hard I had to sit down on a nearby bench and cross my legs to keep from wetting my pants.

The next morning, while Rachel went out alone on her walk through the redneck Chinese gardens, I packed both of our suitcases and threw them into the car. I had a speaking engagement that evening, and I've learned the hard way that it's best not to let Rachel pack her own luggage when we have a schedule to keep. Her detail personality means that while I'm using the wad-'em-up, squish 'em in, sit on it, and zip 'er up method of packing, Rach is folding each pair of her cotton briefs, one pair at a time, into neat little party sandwich shaped bundles. It's enough to give me apoplexy.

Thankfully, Rachel tends to be easygoing in personality, so she didn't mind my headin' us up and movin' us out while she meandered through the fauna and flora around the lake's edge. When I delivered the news that we had to get on the road, Rach followed me to the car, where she saw the humor in yet another detail I'd overlooked.

"Beck," she said, a chuckle rising like soft bubbles to the surface of her voice. "Did you see that sign on our rental car?"

I glanced at it and read out loud, "Monitored by passive security system."

"Now what does that mean?" she mused, sounding like a female Socrates. "Does that mean pacifists are guarding the car? Like if someone tries to steal it, will they hear a recording say, 'Pretty please, we'd like to ask you not to break into this car, for we are peace-loving police and truly wish you no harm. We love you, man. From Your Friendly Neighborhood Passive Security Guards.'"

I laughed so hard I once again had to find a place to park myself and recover. Finally I said, "You're killin' me! That's it.

I'm going to call Jerry Seinfeld and see if you could play his little sister on the show."

"That would be fun," she replied, "but I'd really rather just be your sister because you are one great audience." And I realized, even as Rachel spoke those words, that we'd both always been each other's biggest fans.

I once heard a story about a little girl who came home all excited about her new "part" in the school play. Her mother knew her daughter hadn't won any of the auditions and was both puzzled and curious as she probed for more details. "Tell me more, Sweety. What is your part?"

"Mom," her daughter said with glee, "I've been chosen to clap and cheer!"

When I do well, Rachel claps. When it is her turn to be funny, I cheer. (And laugh, and snort, and look for a place to sit down to recover.) We often play for, and give encouraging feedback to, an audience of one.

And isn't that exactly what sisters do best for each other, after all? Do you have a sister who needs to hear how funny, or smart, or terrific she is? Most of us call our sisters to share our latest news and accomplishments (or heartaches), but perhaps today you could phone a special sister and verbally clap and cheer for her. Every sibling loves a standing ovation. Even if it comes from just one.

We give thanks to God always for you.

1 THESSALONIANS 1:2

8

Warning: My Sister May Self-Destruct

I'm out of my mind; I'll be back in five minutes.
BUMPER STICKER

was on stage in Birmingham, Alabama. My sister was in the audience. I could see her sitting on the third row from the back and drew comfort from her presence though I also felt sorry for her since she'd heard this talk I was about to give at least three times already. But bless her heart, she always laughs and I never once saw her stifle a yawn. So I dove into my routine—funny stories mostly—and then I chatted my way to the poignant section of my speech, verbally and mentally swimming from the shallow to the deeper issues of life—God and the meaning of the universe.

At this point I noticed Rachel covering her mouth. She was laughing! But I wasn't trying to be funny. It was an odd moment, with me on stage continuing to pontificate on the poignant, while at the same time dying to know what she found so comical. Eventually Rachel was so overcome with giggles that she stood up and exited so as not to disturb the audience around her. In addition, there were snickers here and there, like random kernels popping in the audience. A more seasoned speaker now, if this happened again, I would simply stop my speech and ask the audience what was so funny. But I didn't know what to do at the time, so I just plowed on through to the finish line.

After the talk, I immediately found Rachel and asked her, "What was up with the leaving?"

"Becky," she said, struggling to control her laughter and wiping at a tear from the corner of her eye. "Becky," she began again, "while you were speaking so seriously, the big screen that magnified your face malfunctioned. Above your head, in giant red letters, the words 'Warning! Warning!' began blinking. I'm sorry, but I just couldn't help it. I was going to blow! I had to get out of there and get some fresh air to gain control again. You are not only an accident waiting to happen, Becky, you are now coming with your own warning signals."

I know odd things happen to lots of people. Surely they do. But they really do happen with amazing and amusing regularity to me. I've noticed my name has become an adjective among my friends, family, and readers. "Oh, did I ever have a Becky day…" "Let me tell you about my Becky experience…" What follows in their conversation is always some peculiar happening with a funny twist. Several women sent me a true email story the other day about a woman who was having her first mammogram. When the machine appeared to catch fire, incredulously, the attendant left to get help—leaving this poor woman helpless, her breasts smashed and attached to a machine in meltdown. Every email began with some version of, "This sounded to me like this woman was having a real Becky day, and I just had to share it…"

Someone else sent me a commercially sold paper doll named, of all things, "Becky Boo-Boo." Instead of putting paper clothes on her, she comes with a variety of medical supplies: Band-Aids, crutches, a cast.

The doll is only missing one accessory.

Becky Boo-Boo needs a little paper doll sister, named Rachel Rescue, whom she can lean on or at least laugh with when Becky days happen.

○ ○ ○

Two are better than one….For if they fall, one will lift up his companion. But woe to him who is alone when he falls, for he has no one to help him up.

ECCLESIASTES 4: 9-10

9

F ly South for the Winners

*As you may have noticed with some dismay,
most Southerners would rather be charming
than rich. They believe that you can devote
your energies to making money or to being
delightful, but you can't really do both.*

ARTHUR GORDON

One thing I love about talking to women in the South is when
you ask a normal question, the answer you get is usually anything
but normal. As a writer, I love talking to the women of Dixieland
because they give me such original, funny material. If I'm ever
running short of material (which is admittedly rare since my life
is usually a soap opera or sitcom), I can always head south and
ask a few nonchalant questions of women with big hair, bright
pink lips, long manicured nails, and a drawl. Then I get out my
pen and paper pad and write like mad—and usually send a copy

to my sister right away because there's nothing she loves more than a juicy story from a funny Southern female.

Last year I was in Mississippi sitting at a magnolia-covered, church-lady decorated table, chatting it up with the locals between my talks at their ladies retreat. One of the Southern belles said to the other: "Oh, you've gotta tell Becky about your cat in the freezer!" Her friend sheepishly confessed that she'd, just that week, run over her neighbor's cat and killed it. "Since my neighbor is away on vacation, I really didn't know the proper protocol. So I wrapped it up in Saran Wrap and put it in the freezer."

"Oh my..." I said, my eyes widening.

"How awful," empathized another woman.

"But, Honey, you did the right thing, I'm sure," counseled a third.

"I've got a cat in my freezer too!" a fourth woman blurted.

All eyes were now on woman number four as I asked incredulously, "Is there a Southern custom about keeping expired felines in freezers that I've not heard about before?"

"No," she said, eyes cast down. "My cat had kittens last week and when one passed, the doctor suggested I bring it to be autopsied, just to make sure it didn't have a communicable disease that could hurt the other kittens. But his office is closed until Monday, so what could I do?"

In unison, we all said flatly, "Wrap it in Saran, and put it in the freezer."

Honestly, I ask you, do women in Indiana or Michigan have this sort of dinner conversation at church luncheons? And really, what *are* the odds of two women at the same table having a cat in their freezer in Washington or Maine?

But go south, young woman, and anything goes.

One day, a few years back, I was enjoying a glass of lemonade with a group of women from Georgia and one of them asked the other, "How's your broken arm healin', Sugah?"

To which her friend replied, "Much bettuh. Bless your heart for askin'."

I reached right then for my pen and like a professional journalist starving for a story asked, "What happened to your arm?" By now you will realize that if I'd been on the northern half of American soil, the reply would have been something routine like, "I tripped on the ice" or "I fell in the bathroom." It would have been just an answer. When asking such a question of my southern sisters, however, I knew I'd get much more than an answer, I'd get a story. And so the woman across from me took a deep breath to fortify herself as she dove into the "Saga of Her Broken Arm."

"Well, ya see, I was in the doctor's office and this man came in with the cutest little ol' chimpanzee you ever saw."

"A chimp, you say?" I asked, eyebrows raised, trying not to act over-curious so as not to interrupt the story's flow.

"Yes, it was his trained pet. Anyway, I waved at it real friendly like. But I must have accidentally given him the hand signal for 'attack' because the next thing I knew I was pinned to the floor by this chimp who'd suddenly gone wall-eyed nuts. He was on me like a duck on a June bug before I could blink."

"Really?" I probed, my pen gliding across the paper at record speed.

"Yes, Honey. I kid you not. By the time they dragged that monkey off of me, I was bruised all over and my arm was flat *broken*."

See what I mean? The South is a cornucopia of stories just waiting to be told. You may have also observed that many sliceof-life observations do seem a little funnier delivered with a drawl. (Whereas the same story delivered with an English accent tends to make me mentally donate at least 50 extra IQ points to the speaker.) From *Steel Magnolias* to *Designing Women,* there's nothing like a punch line delivered from women with slow-talkin' mouths from the South.

However, there are times when the accent barrier can become a real challenge. Such was the case when my sister and I visited a women's group in Atlanta, where I was to speak that evening. I busied myself setting up the book table and left Rachel alone to mingle with the locals. Rach found a group of women to chat with, and I could tell they were enjoying her as much as she was enjoying them from the laughter that arose from their circle. Within minutes a lovely lady came up to me and drawled, "I like your see-us-ter, Becky. She's real wheeeety."

"She's what?" I asked, not quite comprehending. I translated "see-us-ter" to mean "sister" but I could not for the life of me decipher the rest. Though I did technically live in the South, I really only speak fluent Texan, which is still a couple of states removed from the genteel language of my friends from Mobile and Atlanta.

"She's wheety," the woman repeated, pronouncing the word exactly the same way, but saying it at a slightly faster clip.

Just then Rachel poked her head from behind the woman's shoulder, like the head of a hand puppet, and translated. "Beck, she thinks I'm witty!"

Once I understood, I had to agree with the woman's assessment of my sister's funny bone. In fact, Rachel has now joined the ranks of witty women writers in our family tree with her first book, *Wake Up Laughing,* selling like Alabama hotcakes.

Rachel is on her second book deadline this week, which is the sequel, *Laugh Yourself to Sleep*. As I'm working on this book, we're shooting chapters back and forth over the internet for each other to read and edit. It is so much fun! Should her writing tank ever run low, you can bet my big-sister advice to her will be, "Mosey on down to Mobile or Savannah and sit down among a group of animated women. Preferably ones with big hair, hot pink lipstick, and nails you could dig a ditch with. Then ask a normal question, get your notebook out, and have your pen ready to fly."

*The Lord hath chosen thee to
be a peculiar people...*

Deuteronomy 14:2 KJV

10

Country Mouse/
City Mouse

---

*The difference between landscape
and landscape is small, but there is a
great difference in the beholders.*

EMERSON

Since I've done all the writing about Rachel, I felt it would
be turnabout-is-fair-play and asked her to write about what it is
like to be *my* sister. Remember my recommending taking a trip
to the South with your sister if the two of you should ever get
bored? Well, Rachel looked in her computer archives and found
this travelog of a trip we took together on one of our annual trips
to the land of Dixie about eight years ago.

○ ○ ○

I knew it was going to be an adventure. The phone rang and it was my sister, Becky, who compares herself to Einstein (he was brilliant but never mastered the comb). "Hey, Rach, how'd you like to come to Nashville for four days of R&R? I've got a meeting with my publisher."

It was clear since our childhood days in Texas that Becky and I had a country mouse/city mouse kind of relationship. For 20 years she lived in a small Texas town and eventually made a name for herself as a beloved author and humorist. (I like to call her Erma Bombecky.) During this time I resided in a large Virginia city where I lived for my son's preschool days when I could be alone to sip a stiff cappuccino and hope to just remember my name.

Becky is the ultimate optimist, and I prefer to call myself a realist. She donned her best Vanna voice and began to describe a bed & breakfast she had spotted in a travel book. "It's called the Rose Garden. Guests will enjoy a beautifully appointed 1,000-square-foot suite, private porch with hot tub, fluffy oversized bath towels, and terry cloth bathrobes." Having known friends who have had "interesting" experiences with B&B's, I couldn't help but picture the worst. I imagined a weathered, splintered, wooden porch surrounding a bubbling hot tub teeming with bacteria. Our innkeeper would be the spitting image of Kathy Bates, and we'd be starring in our own version of *Misery. But,* I reasoned, *even if we were staying at the Bates Motel, Becky would find something funny about it and have me rolling in laughter.*

Besides, I'd just survived a "Thirties Transition Year" (Who am I? What am I doing? Who is this guy I married ten years ago? How long have I been this fat and ugly? and so on). I was on the upswing of this premidlife crisis but long overdue for some comic relief. So this city mouse packed her bags and went to see the country mouse.

Becky met me at the gate in Nashville, grinning ear to ear and looking like the Cheshire Cat. The airport seemed strangely subdued to me. Where were the chorus lines of cowgirls in white leather miniskirts and tasseled vests singing, "Welcome to Music City, USA"? Where were the kiosks hawking the world's largest plastic mosquitoes and Conway Twitty hairpieces? To my surprise, I was to learn that this low-key, unassuming atmosphere was pervasive throughout Nashville.

We drove to the Rose Garden, which fortunately lived up to its billing in every way. We were welcomed by a glowing fire in the fireplace, a large overstuffed couch, cherry furnishings, crisp linens, and chocolates on our pillows.

While I poured two mugs of hot herbal tea, Mrs. Trusting Optimist plopped into the hot tub. She was floating around like a happy marshmallow in a vat of hot chocolate. "Come on in, it feels great!" she coaxed. I took a good swift drink of chamomile, threw caution to the wind, and dove in. Tomorrow's headlines flashed through my mind, "SISTERS FOUND DEAD IN LOCAL HOT TUB, CORONER DISCOVERS NEW STRAIN OF E COLI." Actually, it did feel great, and I was comforted by the dense chlorine fumes and the presence of several albino leaves.

○ ○ ○

Laughing at Rachel's perspective of our first evening in Music City, I couldn't help thinking about the old show *The Odd Couple*. Would you like to guess which one of us is Oscar Madison and which is Felix Unger?

And would you like to guess who raced me to the hot tub the next night? We may be an odd couple, but we sure help each other have a good time in this life. What we would have missed without one of us pointing out the lovely details of the wallpaper and the other one plunging headlong into the hot tub with nary a thought of risk!

○ ○ ○

As iron sharpens iron, so a man sharpens the countenance of his friend.

PROVERBS 27:17

11

The Saga of Two Sisters Continues

*Call it charm, call it caring, it's something
we need badly in this mechanized,
fragmented, dehumanized world.*

Arthur Gordon

Having survived the hot tub, Rachel was ready to plan a hot time in the ol' town....I'll let her continue the story of our Big Adventure in Music City, USA, and the lesson she learned that changed her life.

○ ○ ○

We began to plan our schedule for the next three days and were surprised to find that neither of us cared to do any of the usual touristy things. We were both desperate to relax. So we decided to unschedule ourselves and enjoy the local color. However, I really wanted to catch a glimpse of a star (any ol' star would do) and made it clear I would have no pride in pursuing such an endeavor. With that, we threw on our robes and bid each other goodnight.

The next day was rather uneventful, but the evening was memorable. We went to the famous Bluebird Cafe, where aspiring songwriters wait as much as seven months for a chance to perform. The Bluebird was located in a shopping strip off a main road. There were no flashing lights or big signs to mark the spot. Inside the tiny cafe was packed. People smiled and welcomed us. I was struck by the family atmosphere. It seemed so unusual to me having lived so long in a big, impersonal city.

We listened to several promising artists, but the highlight of the evening was a stellar performance by writer Tim Johnson. He penned Mindy McCready's hit "Maybe He'll Notice Her Now." He warmed us up with hilarious themes of living on credit and Stone Age romance, and then went deeper with stealthlike ease. I had stopped laughing, and found my heart pierced with words of passion, faithfulness, and being true to what's really important in life. Teetering on a thin line between maintaining and losing my composure, I was a patsy for his smooth, acoustical style.

It wasn't long before my eyes were stinging, and I felt warm tears trickling down my cheeks. Tim's music and words had hit on something I'd been missing in my life without realizing it. But I was definitely noticing it now.

It was late and we were tired and giddy on the drive back to the Rose Garden. On the previous night, the circular drive had been lit with lantern sacks. But tonight they were conspicuously turned off, causing us to miss our turn. Becky was driving, and said indignantly, "Hey…HEY! They turned off our sacks!" I got really tickled then because her Southern pronunciation of sacks sounded just like you-know-what, and I couldn't resist, "What do you want me to do, go bang on the door and demand sacks?" We laughed so hard we cried.

Somehow we managed to bumble our way onto the drive, where it was clear our innkeepers and their neighbors were sound asleep. The night was so still you could hear a pin drop. We quietly opened our car doors, and Becky began to whisper a story to me about the rudest people she had ever seen. I'm sure what happened next only lasted a few seconds, but it felt like an eternity in slow motion.

As we were getting out of the car, Becky leaned toward my seat to grab a map. She lost her balance and landed on the steering wheel. Let's just say at that moment she literally embodied the phrase "laying on the horn." I was mortified. I ran like a kid from the yard of a freshly toilet papered house when the lights flip on inside.

We woke the next morning (grateful not to have been arrested for disturbing the peace) to a sunlit Tennessee morning. After breakfast, we decided to visit Lepers Fork. (Pronounced "Leapers" Fork. We never asked the origin of the name, but it sounds like they could give Jack Be Nimble a run for his candlestick.) Our mission of leisure was to visit and gather data on a bed & breakfast that had been mentioned in *Southern Living*.

Upon arrival we took in the whole town with one glance. There was a country diner on the left side of the street and a country store on the right. Hungry, we chose the Country Boy Diner, took one step inside the door and several leaps back in time. There was a working soda fountain complete with swivel seats; the walls were paneled wood and furnishings, vintage Formica and vinyl. Upon closer scrutiny I discovered two bulletin boards—the smaller of the two was in an unobtrusive spot near the restrooms. It contained a few autographed photos of country stars. The larger board was placed near the front and was loaded with community news and photos of grandkids. This struck me as a little odd, knowing in the big city I came from the stars would have taken top billing and the grandkids would be lucky to be in a wallet.

Looking around we saw farmers with weathered faces, middle-aged women with tightly permed "do's," and cowgirls wearing blue jeans, pointy boots, and little or no makeup. Everyone seemed at home, and no one seemed to be in a hurry. I found myself envying this laid back, carefree approach to life—free of harried chaos and shallow pretense.

That night I had time to curl up on the fluffy couch at our inn and bask in the warmth of the fireplace, mulling over the day. Everywhere we went we found people who were chatty, who made eye contact, and who seemed genuinely glad to make our acquaintance.

I discovered a name for the ache in my heart, the ache I first felt that night at the Bluebird Cafe. I had been hungry for a *caring community.*

To this day, I still love bright lights and big cities—visiting them, that is. But on this trip to Nashville, my big sister reintroduced me to the real beauty of country-style living: the hearts of the people who live life slow enough to stop awhile, chat, and smile. After a decade in the North, I was homesick for my Southern roots. It took a few years, and a couple of more kids—but eventually I lived in Texas again, within a few country miles of my big sister, Becky.

We laughed the other day as we met for lunch and watched my two baby girls play and had a meal of country-fried catfish and sweet tea together. Becky was about to head north on a business speaking trip. Her children are all nearly raised, and she loves traveling to big cities in faraway places.

And me? I'm happy as a mama duck in a pond with my diaper bag and babies in tow.

Eyeing the two of us together, and the role reversals we've done, our mother summed up the situation beautifully, as only a small town woman could: "Who'd have thunked it?"

○ ○ ○

Every good and perfect gift is from above,
coming down from the Father...

JAMES 1:17

12

Cold Fish, Warm Hearts

*Among those whom I like or admire, I can find
no common denominator, but among those
whom I love, I can: all of them make me laugh.*

W.H. AUDEN

I was out for Mexican food with my mom, my sister, and her growing family. The conversation around the table was typical for the Arnold women—poignant observations peppered with out-loud laughter.

My mother could pass for a comedienne herself. (My kids once saw an episode of the *I Love Lucy Show* when they were little and asked, "Mom? Is that Granny?") However, these days she more often plays a satisfied and easily humored audience to my sister and me.

My humor is typically storytelling in style and self-effacing because nearly all of my anecdotes are about messes I get myself into when I fall on my face. Recently my son informed me that I am a little like every female lead on the show *Friends,* but mostly I remind him of Phoebe. In his words, "You just do and say the most ridiculous, off-the-wall things, but you have absolutely no clue that they are ridiculous or off-the-wall. You live in your own little world, and people can't help but be curious about you. It's sort of like having E.T. as a mother."

Rachel, as I've noted, has a dry, sharp, observational humor that punctuates the air out of nowhere, leaving everyone around her chuckling and intrigued by her unique point of view.

But back to the enchiladas at hand. I opened the conversation at the restaurant table with my latest tale of being on the road speaking. While in a strange city, I'd bit into an apple and lost a good size chunk of one of my front teeth. Since I was appearing on a television show the next day, I ended up driving around town begging for help from dentist to dentist to find someone who could see me before closing time.

"What did you say to get them to help you?" Mom asked.

Before I could answer, my sister piped up, "Well, Mom, I'm pretty sure Becky probably said, 'Pleath, pleath, can you fixth my tooth!'" As the laughter around the table began to die down, the waitress came up to take our orders.

I chose something I thought would win the admiration of my health-conscious mother: orange roughy with tomatoes and green onions and avocado slices. I pictured it served Mexican style—simmering on a fajita-type plate surrounded by appropriate garnishes. So did everyone else in the family.

When the actual dish arrived, however, we were all caught off guard. My eight-year-old nephew's eyes grew enormous as he looked from the entrée on the waitress' tray to my eyes and back again, waiting for what I might say about this newly presented predicament. What my meal turned out to be was raw fish (I'm assuming it was orange roughy) chopped up and poured into a tall parfait dish, with the tomatoes, avocado, and green onions layered like fudge, nuts, and whipped cream. It was, by all appearances, a cold fish sundae. (Though I have since learned from some fellow "foodies" that cerveche is supposed to be served raw. It's sort of south-of-the-border style sushi.)

"What's this?" I asked the waitress, trying not to act shocked.

Rachel was quick to supply the answer. She may move slowly in the details category, but she's fast with a comeback. "Beck, looks to me like *this*—is Fish in a Dish."

My nephew, Trevor, chimed in, "Yeah—fish in a dish, Aunt Becky!"

Rachel leaned over to deadpan yet another word of explanation. "I believe they call it the Dr. Seuss Special."

Even the waitress couldn't help but grin. (And bless her heart, she kindly exchanged my order for something more well done…and less bait-like.)

Often when Rachel and I are together I feel like we're in a walking, breathing, sister sitcom. A sister lightens every emotional load we carry. Sometimes it is by bringing the cheesecake and a box of Kleenex and crying with us. But just as often it is with the simple gift of a shared laugh…be it over one fish, two fish, red fish…or cold fish.

Then our mouth was filled with laughter.

Psalm 126:2

13

Of Surrogate Sisters & Leftover Meatballs

A listening ear, a supportive comment, a caring heart touches an ache within that continuing on responsibly doesn't quite relieve. We value the encouragement that occurs when something uniquely human comes out of another person and into us.

LARRY CRABB

Becky, I have a favor to ask you." The voice on the other end of the phone was that of my dear, very pregnant friend Lindsey O'Connor.

"Anything!" I offered. Who can deny a friend any request in her ninth month?

"You've got a deadline; I've got a deadline. I'm miserable—burning up in this August heat, and I know you must be overheating down there in Texas. Our friend Vicki has offered to let us stay in her air-conditioned home in Colorado Springs for a week while she's on vacation."

"Say no more! Sounds like a dream. I'll pack my bags and book a flight."

As I would eventually write in the foreword to the book Lindsey would finish up that week,

> Thus began one of the most idyllic weeks of writing and friendship I've ever enjoyed. In fact, I've never spent an entire week alone with a writing friend—focusing only on writing, prayer, soul-sharing, and eating out, all done at a leisurely pace. It was a true oasis of the heart for both of us in a year that has just about "done us in." I was reminded of the week Anne Morrow Lindbergh spent at a beach house with her sister, away from husband, kids, phone, and demands. They'd visit and share breakfast in the morning, taking lingering walks along the ocean's shore, then close the doors as they each tended to their own projects during the day, uninterrupted—a luxury in and of itself. Then, as evening drew near, they'd gather to share the day's writing produce, along with a simple meal. The result of that week was a *Gift from the Sea,* a classic book for women about simplicity and slowing down to the heartbeat of life. (From the Foreword to Lindsey's book *If Mama Goes South, We're All Going with Her.*)

I watched Lindsey fill up her thirsty soul in our week together as she sat on the back porch in view of the mountains, poring over

Scriptures, jotting notes to her heart's content, truly as happy as I've ever seen her. Wordlessly, we worked out a system where I'd bring her hot coffee in the morning, and she'd pour me something cool to drink in the late afternoon. Sometimes we'd eat in; often we'd venture out for a meal; more often we'd end up driving in circles, lost but laughing aloud, both of us hopelessly directionally impaired. And though she was close to the end of her pregnancy and in terrible back pain, she was incredibly kind to me during this week. She literally cried tears over the heartaches I'd suffered in a pain-filled year, holding my hand and praying for me. And when I needed to make a difficult decision, she spoke words so profound that I looked into her luminous dark eyes and asked when she'd become so wise.

Pause with me here for a moment. Can we talk? Having a wise friend isn't always a picnic. I must admit that Lindsey has been unfailingly forthright with me at times when I didn't want to hear it. In fact, we recently had a conversation at her kitchen counter about this very subject, marveling at not only the crises our friendship has survived but also the conflicting opinions and emotions we've weathered. And yet we've come out of all the storms not only stronger as individuals, but stronger as friends.

"Why do you think you were able to handle my telling you the truth even when it could have pushed you away?" she asked, dipping a piece of French bread into some wonderful herbal-olive oil concoction she saved just for this afternoon visit.

"Because I know it took courage."

"It did! I had to take such a risk that I might lose you as a friend if I held out for what I felt deep in my heart was the truth."

"I know. And there's something else. I once heard you should never tell someone a hard truth unless it truly pains you to do so. In your case, I always knew this was true."

She smiled in response and nodded. Lindsey's nature is to please, but her sense of truth is never subservient to her innate kindness. I know it just about killed her the few times she felt she had to "speak the truth in love." And I also know she's never spoken a difficult word to me that wasn't bathed in prayer, given hours of thought, and often sustained by deep spiritual study. Any difficult opinions have always been given with my best interest truly at heart.

I wrote Lindsey not long ago to tell her that her example of integrity, mingled with compassion, makes me want to be a better woman. As "iron sharpens iron," as Solomon said, so does one man (or woman) sharpen another.

Somewhere, probably beginning in that idyllic writing week followed by a series of unbelievable traumas complete with compassion and truth-telling, our relationship shifted from friendship to something that feels a lot more like sisterhood.

In fact, my sister and I recently voted to adopt Lindsey as our third sister. To being with, Lindsey doesn't have a sister of her own, and her own mother passed away when Linds was just in her thirties, so she's rather bereft of females in her family tree. (However she's birthed four daughters of her own, thus ensuring she'll have plenty of female-bonding opportunities in her future.) She also looks like one of us. Like my sister and I, she has medium-length dark hair and brown eyes. We've decided to forgive the fact that she's about a thousand pounds lighter than us since she likes Mexican food and is a great conversationalist. (Though I must admit to trying to fatten her up so she'll blend with our clan a bit better. I once shared our sisterly secret with her: When you pass Krispy Kreme and the "hot" light is on, it means that it is God's will to stop and eat at least two warm, sugary doughnuts, guilt free.)

Considering that Lindsey is about the size of a coffee stirrer, it is amazing how many of our best bonding moments happen over food. Most of our lunches out and evening dinner dates are to celebrate the everyday joys of life: our kids, our careers, our euphoria at getting to indulge in enchiladas and uninterrupted chick-chat for an hour. Especially wonderful has been sharing the big-life events, such as when my husband Greg and I danced at her eldest daughter's storybook wedding. Jacquelyn (who is often mistaken for Catherine Zeta Jones) and her husband, Noah, an air force officer in full dress uniform, could have been models for *Bride Magazine.* Then there was Lindsey in all her glory: her dark hair piled up in an elegant twist, her high cheekbones, her thousand-watt smile, dressed to the nines in her bronzy-gold 1940's style gown, looking as though she'd spent most of her life eating bon-bons and instructing the servants as to where to put her breakfast tray. On the arm of her handsome hero-husband, Tim, they rivaled the bride and groom for romance personified.

Savoring the fruited pork loin and sipping the wedding punch to the smooth and peppy sounds of Sinatra, I couldn't help but compare this joyous occasion to the Worst of Times—when this wonderful friend was near death, in a coma for months following childbirth, with no happy ending in sight. (Yes, that occurred shortly after that Most Idyllic Writing Week. Life is, as they say, mundane or lovely seasons punctuated by moments of sheer terror.)

Greg and I met with Tim at a restaurant after visiting Lindsey's almost lifeless body in the hospital, following the birth of her last child, Caroline, born healthy and beautiful to a mother who went almost immediately into serious trauma. Between dipping chips into salsa, we pondered the crisis at hand and wondered how life could keep going, clocks could keep ticking, Tim could keep breathing, and the family could still put one foot in front of the other. We were all painfully short on answers but overflowing with questions. We were simply hanging on for dear life to our faith, to each other…to the semi-normalcy of mindlessly dipping chips into salsa. Looking across the table at Tim's red-rimmed eyes, I don't remember the taste of chips and salsa as much as I do the taste of salty tears on my tongue. We gathered together as much for emotional nourishment as physical sustenance, which is, I imagine what "supping together" has implied through the centuries.

Eventually the story had a happy ending. Lindsey got well and, thankfully, since that scary season, most of our meals together have been celebratory in nature again. Even the smallest joys seem worth toasting when you've been given a second chance at life. However, life being life, there are still those awful days that hit our families now and again. Recently it was the O'Connor household that was blindsided by an unforeseen tragedy. Greg and I again drove to meet Tim and Lindsey at a restaurant. There they were, zoned out, and numbly dipping chips into salsa. We slid into the seats, and I reached out to pat Lindsey's hand. I said, "Here we are, in crisis together again."

Tim looked up, his eyes glazed with pain, and said, "We've got to stop meeting like this."

That did it. We broke into laughter, at which point Lindsey said, "This is the first time I've laughed in three days. It feels so good."

I nodded. "Reminds me of my favorite line from *Steel Magnolias:* 'Laughter through tears is my favorite emotion.'"

"Becky brought you something," Greg reminded.

I handed her a Tupperware container. "I never quite know what to do in a crisis, but show up and bring food. But I didn't have time to cook anything, so here's some pretty good leftover meatloaf."

She laughed and took the container. I shook my head and said, "Have you seen that movie *The Wedding Singer?* In it this adorable little old woman pays for her singing lessons with food. She just ladles a meatball covered with sauce into the guy's bare hands, without benefit of napkin or plate. Well, that's what I feel like right now. Like I'm giving you a meatball in your outstretched hands. It's not much, but it's all I have at the moment."

Lindsey smiled. "Instead of a cup of cold water in Jesus' name..."

"...Yeah, it's a meatball in His name."

More cleansing laughter through tears.

The next day I got an email from Lindsey...

> When you and Greg made us laugh in that restaurant, it was the first time we'd laughed since this began. It shocks you at first! And then the sweetness of it fills you, and you realize that you will not die. Not at that moment anyway. Your meatloaf was as good as being handed a meatball in the palm. :) I had thirty minutes to be with Alli and Caroline before a meeting tonight, so I forced myself to talk in that tone of voice meant to comfort and soothe and calm, praying it sounded more real to them than it did to me, [which was] like a bad actor. We cooked carrots to go with your meatloaf because that seemed like an ordinary thing to do. A normal thing to do together. "Girls,

do you want to cook carrots with Mommy?" Oh yes they did. So man, we cooked carrots. Then we sat down and ate at the table, a normal moment amidst hardship. Thank you for all the meatballs you've given us along the way, my friend. They comfort me as does your friendship.

They say that 90 percent of success in life is just showing up. Ninety percent of friendship—or better yet, surrogate sisterhood—is also just showing up. The other 10 percent is bringing a meatball.

(Needless to say, with our track-records of traumas and multiple children, we've decided to start stockpiling meatballs.)

We are sort of swimming our way through a muddy river called life. Then you find Jesus, and He's like this log you can heave yourself onto, get your head out of the mud, and breathe some fresh air. And then, once you are able, you help others onto the log—but basically we're all just clinging to the log for dear life. None of us any better than the other. We don't completely escape the muddy river either. It taints us and soils us and tries to pull us down…and sometimes it succeeds. But by clinging to each other, and the log that is Christ, we'll make it to the other side.

HUGH HALTER (my pastor)

The Sisterhood Rules

In pondering what traits take a woman from being a good friend to being a surrogate sister, I thought of my friendship with Lindsey and came up with these five right away.

1. You are gut-wrenchingly honest with each other, never compromising your personal standards of integrity—but gently so, sandwiching criticism with praise because you've loved each other unconditionally over a long period of time, through a variety of circumstances: good, bad, and ugly.

   Lindsey's insistence on personal and professional integrity in all things, down to the smallest detail, has been frustrating at times, but I hear her voice in my head every time I'm tempted to take shortcuts or a wrong turn, and it sounds an awful lot like the message the Holy Spirit is whispering in my other ear.

   In turn, I think my laid-back easygoing, "just play the melody" nature has helped Lindsey accept some of the joys of imperfection.

2. You've been loyal as Labradors to each other, refusing to gossip or share confidences with others when one or the other is going through a rough patch or a temporary insanity.

3. You understand when to cry with her and when to help her laugh off a bad day.

4. You applaud each other in all of life's highpoints and accomplishments, even if she *is* prettier or thinner or deeper than you are. Because, after all, her joy is yours, as are her sorrows—and you know the reverse is also true.

5. You give each other lots of "grace space," meaning you

aren't easily offended by someone running late, or a small misunderstanding, or difference of opinion. Lindsey has five children and a schedule that is hectic beyond comprehension. At this season of her life, if at all possible, I try to make it easy on her to get together. I drive near where she's picking up a kid from school or hold our "lunch time" schedule loosely (bringing a good book or a manuscript to edit) knowing she's juggling several kids to get free to see me. Lindsey's also generous with grace space when I'm running late—even though I don't have the excuse of five kids at home…I'm just organizationally challenged.

There is no better friend than a great sister. And there is no better sister than a great friend.

14

Of Trapezes and Birthdays

With the fearful strain that is on me night and day, if I did not laugh I should die.

ABRAHAM LINCOLN

In searching old emails I found the following dialogue written around my birthday on April 16, 1999. I did know that this was my birthday, but when I hit age 30, I simply stopped keeping track of how old I was. A group of friends wanted to honor my birthday, and Rachel was desperately trying to determine my real age for the occasion.

From: Rachel
Subject: Let me outta this gene pool!

Becky, I'm laughing my head off. I have to pass on this message I just wrote to Mom.
Love,
Little Sister Who AT LEAST Knows How Old She IS

From: Rachel
To: Mom and Dad
Date: Monday, April 10, 2000 4:11 PM
Subject: How old IS Becky?

I'm laughing. Lynn M. orchestrated a neat, personalized gift for Becky from her writer friends (most of whom she's helped break into the business). Lynn asked me if this was Becky's 40th, and I said "yes." Later I checked with niece Rachel Praise and she said, "Hey, you're a year late. Mom turned 40 last year, but no matter, she forgets who she is and how old she is half the time anyway."

Today, we get an effusive email of thanks from Becky stating, "You really made turning 42 so much easier." I'm laughing again just thinking of this fiasco! Will the real Age of Becky please stand up? DO YOU KNOW HOW OLD YOUR OLDEST DAUGHTER IS? Can you check the birth certificate?

Mystified in Georgia,
Rachel, born Jan. 3, 1964 (I think…)

To: Rachel
From: Becky

Subject: Mystery Solved

> I was born in 1959. I've recalculated that figure
> and have determined I am actually 29 years old.
> And holding. <grin>

As you've plainly seen, though Rachel is my younger sister, she's often had to play a big sister role in my life by reminding me where I am, what I'm doing, and how old I am. One horrible year (the year I really think I deserved at least a T-shirt for surviving), Rachel also took on the task of reminding me *who* I was. In a shocking and devastating year, I lost my marriage of 27 years, went to three funerals of close friends or family members, and felt I might always be stuck in grief with no possible hope for a normal future. So many times during that season of sorrow, I counted on Rachel to call me back from the edges of insanity and pain. Where would we be without our sisters when our world, as we know it, falls apart?

After holding my hand through that horrible year, Rachel witnessed my finally turning an emotional corner toward hope and happiness. It was April, and spring was greening its way through the drab of winter. It was also my birthday again, and I was turning 44—I think. My sister and her family and my parents met for a weekend in Sundance Square, a lovely restored and upgraded section of downtown Fort Worth. (A city the locals call "Cow Town.") My family had gathered 'round to help celebrate my own greening again, the small but significant signs that life could be good again.

There's a book out now called *Between Trapezes,* and if ever there was a good metaphor for what it feels like to be in a time of transition, that's a great one. I had let go of the trapeze of my old familiar life, and now I was in flight, midair, reaching toward the next trapeze, trusting that God would catch me somewhere out there in the dark. It was terrifying, but also exhilarating.

After a wonderful meal, Rach and I strolled along the cobblestone streets lined with trees that were covered in sparkling golden lights. The buildings surrounding us were tall and sleek and lit up, beautiful and promising, against the warm, spring sky. We reached a corner and I looked up, smiled, held out both of my arms and spun around like a little girl.

As if on cue, Rachel began to sing the theme song from the old Mary Tyler Moore Show: "Who can turn the world on with her smile…"

I grinned and spontaneously picked up the next line and sang it back to my sister, "Who can take a nothing day…"

Together we locked arms, strode forward, and let the rest of the song rip, as passersby stared at us like the two crazy women we are.

We garnered one smile and a little applause from a bellboy standing outside a hotel.

But I felt a smile from heaven beaming down on two sisters who, together, were finding the path back to life again.

I love you, Rachel. Thank you for singing my song back to me, when I could not remember the words anymore.

○ ○ ○

Oddly enough as I update this chapter today, I glanced at the calendar and realized my birthday is coming up in four days. Since that day in Sundance Square, when my life was literally up in the air, I've finally landed on another trapeze. I could not have fathomed it at the time, but this trapeze I'm now on is the most beautiful, happy one imaginable. I am now remarried to an unbelievably precious man who loves me so tenderly it brings tears of joy to my eyes almost daily. Greg and I live in Colorado—the most beautiful state in the union. My yard is aflame with yellow daffodils and red tulips, and purple mountain majesties surround us everywhere we look. Most of my children now live here too, plus I've inherited two amazing stepsons. And I'm expecting my first grandchild. I love my church, my home, my career…my life. I don't think I've ever been this happy in my life (and I've had my share of happiness). I don't think I realized that a human being could actually experience this much joy on a continual basis.

Glancing once more at the calendar I see that my birthday falls on Easter Sunday this year—resurrection morning. I just got a call from my father who sent my sister and me an email of joy today. My mother has been tending to my father's sister, who is suffering from cancer and also from a crisis of faith. She's been a self-made woman all her life, kindly of heart, but believing Christians to be naïve, and religion is the "opium of the masses." It turns out that she's hungry for some of that "opium" for the soul in her hour of suffering with eternity lying open before her. Besides lovingly tending to her physical needs, Mother is tending to her soul. She prayed with my aunt last night and saw her gratefully accept Christ's offer of forgiveness, of peace, of eternal life. "Hear the bells ringing? They're singing that we can be born again!" Even if death should come, she now knows it is only a passage to another kingdom more beautiful than our minds can comprehend.

My reading friend, my soul sister out there, are you "between trapezes" right now? Do you wonder if there's any chance of springtime ever returning to your heart? If you don't have a sister to remind you of who you are and of the good things in store, let me be your sister for a moment. Let me be His love and encouragement to you today. As one famous preacher used to say, "Today may be Friday…but Sunday's coming!" No matter how bad you feel today, how hopeless things may seem…even if the worst should be happening, something more than a temporary crisis…even if you are battling cancer or a life-threatening illness…you *will* rise again to see better days because Christ rose to give you new life.

Hang on to Him, Sister! You're gonna make it after all.

Forget the former things; do not dwell on the past. See, I am doing a new thing! Now it springs up; do you not perceive it?

ISAIAH 43:18 NIV

15

Shared Sorrow
Is Half a Sorrow

A wounded deer—leaps highest.
EMILY DICKINSON

Perhaps the reason Rachel knew, instinctively, how to comfort me in my year of sorrow, was that she too passed through a time when it seemed the sun would never shine. You've read of her meticulous, things-under-control personality in this volume. For a time, she was allowed to live under the illusion that life was somehow controllable and manageable.

For many years Rachel lived a pretty halcyon existence in a nice, neat Virginia neighborhood, with a nice, neat husband with a nice, neat job. Together they raised one nice, neat child, Trevor. She drove every morning to a nice, neat coffee shop and upon the first sip of her steaming latte would say a prayer of thanks for her nice, neat life. And then her nice, neat husband lost his nice, neat job to a nasty, messy corporate takeover.

And that's when the threads of all-she'd-once-counted-on began unwinding, one by one.

After a year of job searching in a too-crowded field, my sister and her little family had to sell their home and store everything that had given her surroundings familiarity. With heartbreaking resignation, they had to move from beautiful Virginia to the flatlands of Texas to live with our parents for a few months while her husband continued the search for work. Emails from Rachel during that period were especially poignant. My funny sister was hurting, and I ached along with her.

One day she wrote, "You know, Beck, sometimes I wonder if down the road I'll be 'glad' in a sad kind of way about all we've been through. For example, let's just say that you help me get a book contract, and we sell billions and billions of copies. To be honest with you (and I'm tearing up as I contemplate this), I'm not sure I would ever look back and say, 'O.K., this was worth going through that.' Do you know what I mean? I feel at this moment that I will always look back on this time as very painful, demoralizing, and scary. Not to say that I won't see the silver linings, but I guess I feel that when my life is over I'll just think, 'There were some very special times, but also some very painful times, and now it's over.'"

Thankfully a reprieve came in the form of freelance work in Atlanta, but Rachel, like Tigger, had lost her bounce. When her young son, Trevor, would try to be tougher than the lump forming in his throat, and when he'd lose the battle and cry out in pain for his old life, his old friends, and his old school, Rachel thought her heart might not bear it.

Some days she'd draw strength from God's Word, some days she'd feel that He was playing tricks with her hopes. Some days she didn't have the strength to think or feel at all: She was doing good to just get up, move slowly and achingly through the day, and pray that the earthquake that had wrecked her nice, neat life would soon be over.

Eventually the freelance assignment took on more permanent proportions, and the little family moved to Atlanta to an apartment that overlooked a comforting lake. As Rachel began to gather some of her own familiar pots and pans and pictures into the apartment and sat by the window and watched the leaves turn from summer green to rich, fall colors of orange and red and yellow, hope began to raise its tired head once again. Small joys—like great writing assignments and positive comments from editors and our sister getaway trips—were also helpful.

It was about this time that Rachel discovered she was pregnant again, after eight years of mothering an only child. She couldn't believe it, so she kept quiet about it until she was four months along.

"How could you not tell me?" I asked the evening she spilled the baby beans.

"Because I was embarrassed," she answered honestly. "We're out of work. This is not a good time to have a baby. I can't even control my birth control anymore!"

In the book *The Sacred Romance,* Brent Curtis and John Eldridge speak of our human desire to have a Less Wild Lover than the real God happens to be. We want a Nice Guy God who plays by the rules. We behave, He blesses us. No big surprises. But the authors admit the truth: Knowing God often feels more like having that crazy Mel Gibson character from the Lethal Weapon movies as your partner.

Why? Because He is not going after our comfort. This Wild Lover of ours is coming after our hearts. One way He does this is to remind us that we are not in control. Life cannot be managed. It can only be fully lived with all its sorrow and joy and uncertainty. Seasons come and go—some filled with happiness, some with tears. No matter the season, there is only one constant: the presence of God, the Wild Lover of our Souls, in the midst of it all. And it is only by surviving such seasons that we really discover the truth: He is enough. He'll take care of us.

Rachel's season of suffering lasted three long, hard years. But at the end of those years this woman who could not control life was gifted with not one, but *two* baby girls within the next three years. The Lord provided in a miraculous way for their physical needs, so much so that she's been able to be especially generous to the needs of others, including me, this year. She moved to Texas, nearer family and is making good friends, finding her place in the sun.

And though Rachel may not realize it, the best gift she received was a new tenderness of heart, a deeper compassion for others who suffer, and a profound spirit of gratitude for all good things that come our way. My little sister grew up in those three years in ways she could not have grown by any other means.

I was privileged to suffer alongside and help, when I could, to ease Rachel's pain in her trials. She has been there in abundance for me as I've weathered my painful months.

For sisters are not only there to "double your pleasure and double your fun," as the Doublemint twins sing. Sisters are here to share our sorrows when they become too heavy to carry alone.

○ ○ ○

Come to me, all you who are weary and burdened, and I will give you rest.

MATTHEW 11:28 NIV

16

Puppy Love and Kitty-Cat Cuddles

Sisters are different flowers from the same garden.
BECKY FREEMAN JOHNSON

True confession: I have the two cutest nieces in the whole world. Not surprisingly, they are the offspring of my own cutest little sister in the world.

Tori, age five, is a delicate child, willowy and prone to daydreaming. Her large, expressive, "Audrey Hepburn" eyes peer out at the world in wonder beneath the wispy bangs of her short bob. She's like a kitten who sidles up to you only when you aren't looking or, heaven forbid, focusing on her. She is sublimely subtle in her style of affection, preferring "by-the-way" terms of endearment. Read her a book she loves and you'll find that almost imperceptibly, her tiny hand is resting tenderly on your arm, stroking it softly. I half-expect her to purr. Or engage her in baking a batch of cookies, and from her perch on the stepstool, she'll gently lean her head against your side, look up and offer you a shy and happy smile.

Tori's little sister, Whitney, at age three, is a sturdier child. Though she and Tori share the same soft-brown, pageboy bobs, Whitney is a cuddle-pack who runs and jumps at you with playful puppy love, her yip-yapping heart on her sleeve. There's not a shy bone in Whitney's body. (In fact she's so soft and huggable, I sometimes wonder if there are any bones in Whit's body.) She came into her own outgoing personality when President George W. Bush was in his presidential prime. Bumper stickers (usually on the back of pickup truck windows) were proclaiming "Vote for W" everywhere you looked, especially in our home state of Texas. So we took to calling Whitney, "Dubya," and she's been glad-handing and charming her public like a miniature Southern politician ever since.

Last summer Greg and I picked up my sister's clan at the Denver airport. To our delight they'd decided to vacation in and around Colorado and make our house homebase for a week. Trevor, my now 13-year-old nephew, who has the patience of a monk and the talent of Billy Crystal, was entertaining his little sisters to keep them from drifting into whine mode—to his mother's everlasting gratitude. Trev has always called me Crazy Aunt Becky, as if it were one name: Crazyauntbecky. But I know he loves me because he's inherited the Arnold family legacy: the intense desire to make others laugh that overcomes any natural tendency to be seen as normal or even cool. This week he is playing the starring role in his school's play, *The Pink Panther*, garnering rave reviews with his dead-on imitation of Inspector

Clouseau. But I digress. (And yes, I bragged. Indulge me—I'm a proudandcrazyaunt!)

When Whitney saw us she practically leaped into my arms with a torrent of words describing the "ayapwane" and the salty cereal snacks and the cold cup of "Spwite" and the fluffy white "cwouds" and how she was SO happy to be here and loved us all SO much. In fact, she loved everybody in the whole airport. But Tori, typically, demurred—until I pretended to not really notice her, and by and by, I felt her soft little hand in mine, her inaudible purr of affection at my side.

We drove them to our home in Denver, and immediately the girls wanted to inspect the room where they'd be sleeping. As a surprise I'd purchased each a brightly colored knit short set, laying them out on the bed. Whitney was immediately seized by uncontrollable gratitude and ecstasy, jumping on the mattress as she held up her present, a shirt in one hand and a pair of shorts wadded up in the other fist, gleefully exclaiming, "Purple is my most favorite color! I LOVE this outfit! I think it is the pwettiest shirt and shorts I ever saw. Can I put them on now? Can I sleep in them? Thank you, Aunt Becky and Uncle Greg!"

I glanced over at the foot of the bed and spied Tori carefully holding her new duds, her eyes wide as she carefully examined each seam, the pink of the fabric—a shy smile of approval slowly spreading across her face. Then she simply held the clothes to her chest, and let out a slow but dramatic sigh of joy.

The next morning I whipped up a breakfast fit for two miniature princesses: homemade blueberry waffles. The girls looked so cute at the little table and chair set I bought them, dipping pieces of waffle into little bowls of syrup, the sun shining in through the kitchen windows haloing their heads.

Whitney, who feared no man, took no time in bonding with her new "Uncle Gweg." Later that day Greg went out to the back porch and sat in a lounge chair to enjoy the cool summer breeze. Whitney soon spotted and joined him. I heard Greg lean over to Whitney and say generously, "Whitney, tell me about anything you want to talk about. I'm here to listen." Thirty minutes later, I looked out on the patio and Whitney was still looking earnestly at Greg, talking 90 miles a minute, her hands flying to further emphasize her many and varied points. I opened the back door to check on their progress. Greg looked up at me and said, "I've heard women need to say 20,000 words per day. I think Whitney is on about 25,000 and counting. Apparently she had a lot stored up today."

So enamored was Whitney of Greg that from that moment on, she insisted on sitting by him often and exclusively using "Uncle Gweg's" potty (in our upstairs master bathroom). One late night my sister found her leaning against our closed bedroom door.

"What are you doing, Honey?" Rachel asked.

"I'm just waiting for Uncle Gweg to wake up," she said. "I need to talk to him."

The next day, in her own way, Tori quietly expressed her affection for Uncle Greg by drawing a picture of him (which is still on our fridge). Not only did she draw his moustache and goatee (with an orange crayon to reflect his red hair), she even colored in the space between Greg's front teeth.

Watching these sisters express their love and gratitude in such different, but equally delightful ways, I couldn't help but wonder if God looks at His children lovingly from on high, enjoying the variety of ways they express their gratitude. Just like kids opening presents on Christmas morning, some Christians are beside themselves with joy—hopping, skipping, shouting, hands lifted in excitement. Others open their gifts and simply stare with a quiet awe and wonder, taking time to absorb everything about it—noticing, appreciating, turning the present over and over in their hands. Both types must make the Father's heart ache with love and tenderness.

The next morning I woke up to a little round face peering over the edge of my mattress. Though she was still in her jammies and had a pacifier stuffed in her mouth, "Dubya's" eyes were wide and alert. Though the pacifier muffled her voice, I was able to understand everything she said, all too well. Without fanfare, or introduction, or as much as a "good morning, howdy-do," Whitney dove in with her morning's instructions. "Aunt Becky, I want you to get up and make me waffles. With bwuberries. I want the waffles squauh, not round. I want you to cut it in little pieces, and I want to dip it in a bowl of sywup. And I want some bacon and owange juice too. That's all." It sounded exactly like a child version of Meg Ryan's famous picky and complicated cafe order in the movie *When Harry Met Sally.*

I wiped the sleep from my eyes and stumbled downstairs toward the coffeemaker and the waffle iron, with a cheerfully chatting cherub toddling expectantly behind me. As I pulled a hot waffle out of the iron and began cutting it into little pieces as directed, I felt a slight pressure on my leg. Looking down, I saw Tori standing there, leaning, fragile with morning grogginess, in her pink princess nightie.

"Would you like a waffle too?" I asked.

She nodded silently in the affirmative, rubbing her eyes.

While Whitney happily and noisily chatted about anything and everything to anyone and no one, getting a good morning's start on her daily word count, I bent down and hugged Tori and whispered softly that I loved her.

Then she smiled, laid her sleepy head on my shoulder, and purred.

○ ○ ○

As a father has compassion on his children, so the LORD has compassion on those who fear him.

PSALM 103:13 NIV

17

Sister Rivalry

Sister to sister we will always be, a
couple of nuts off the family tree.
AUTHOR UNKNOWN

One of my uncles used to refer to a pair of outgoing and mischievous twin sisters in his neighborhood as "The Sin Twisters." As wonderful as sisterly love may be, it is not without its "sin twister" moments. Anyone who has raised multiple daughters or who grew up in a house with a sister or two (or more) knows something of the competition, the petty jealousies, the one-up-on-her-ship that is a part of female siblings living in close quarters, sharing one bathroom mirror.

I've noticed that sisterly rivalry is especially true of siblings who are close in age and had to share a room. My sister's little girls, Tori and Whitney, fall into that category with only a few cushioning years between them. They don't share a room, but they are in each other's "space" quite a bit and the result is lots of high-pitched squealings of frustration. And at this young age and stage—Tori is five, Whitney, age three—they are not above putting down the other sister in order to make themselves look good to mom or dad.

When the girls were here over this summer, they loved to have me roll down the window in the car so they could put their hands out in the breeze as we drove along. I allowed it only for the slow drive down our residential street, knowing it would be too dangerous once we got into traffic.

Before I could get out of the driveway, however, Whitney lost it. "I want you to roll down the window right now!"

"Just a minute, Whit," I said, "I have to get the car backed out first."

But alas, Whit was tired and cranky, in desperate need of a nap, and no amount of logic could appease her. She wanted the window down, and she wanted it down now, with no guff from the grownups in the front seat.

At this point, I heard Tori's voice sounding especially angelic coming from her car seat next to Whitney's in the back. "I'm not whining. I'm being patient."

"Yes, you are," my sister and I agreed.

"But Whitney is being bad and cranky and whining. She's not being patient at all, is she?"

My sister caught the one-up-on-her-sister direction that Tori was heading and said, "Tori, I'm glad you are being good. But you need to let me correct Whitney. I do not need you to point out that she's being whiney. That's between mommy and Whit."

"Yeth," lisped Whitney in utter exasperation. "Besides, I wasn't whining. I was being therious!"

Rachel and I caught each other's eyes and we were goners, laughing so hard we nearly cried. One thing all of our kids have learned about their mamas, right or wrong: If you can make us laugh you have doubled your chances of escaping being in therious trouble.

For the most part, I think my sister and I escaped the normal sibling squabbles because there are five years between us, we each had our own bedrooms, and by the time she was 12 years old, I was out of the house and married. Plus we're both pretty laid-back, nonconfrontive types by nature. Even though we're both writers, there's amazingly no feeling of competition between us. We're just excited about each other's success.

When it came time for Rachel to try her writing wings, she wanted to make sure she landed a book contract on her own merit and not on the short coattails of my semi-success or that of my mother's. She went to great lengths not to use our names in her proposal, and to her credit, she made it into publishing all on her own. And her first book was a raving success. And she did it all by herself, thankyouverymuch. (Actually, having read this paragraph, Rachel would like to balance this by saying that I DID give her a boatload of encouragement to write the book in the first place, and that our mother and a dear friend Lynn Morrissey were kind enough to read over the manuscript and edit the final draft. I guess there's not a writer out there who can claim total solo achievement. Even the most experienced writers accept critique…and even seek it out.)

Anyway, now that she's achieved the validation she wanted and needed, Rachel's singing a more relaxed and different tune.

My husband is now her agent, and she, Mom, and I are all writing and helping each other in any way possible, from edits to endorsements to networking—hang the coattails! The last time Rachel and her husband were visiting us, Greg and I talked about her future career direction over dessert and coffee.

"Look," Rachel said, "I wrote my last book without using any of my family's literary ties to get my foot in the door. I did well; the book did well. I feel good about that. But I'd really like a bigger advance the next time so I can justify the time it takes away from my kids to write a book. I'd like to hire some household help as well to lower the stress level."

"And so," Greg said, "is it okay that I, as your brother-in-law and agent, use Becky's name or your mom's as endorsements on the proposal? The reason it might be handy is that your sister or your mom's name may be familiar to other publishers and might make it a bit easier to get you in the door of some new houses. Think about it: A family of lawyers often spawn more lawyers, and most teachers had a mom or dad who had a career in teaching. The same is true for writers: Good ones often don't fall far from some sort of literary family tree. Your Aunt Etta, your mom, and your sister have all been writers. It only makes sense that you'd someday take up the feminine writing pen. And it wouldn't surprise me if one of your daughters follows suit someday. Think of the Bronte sisters, who probably happily climbed up on each other's petticoats and turned that sisterly synergy into a family powerhouse of publishing. Of course, at the end of the day, it will be your writing and your excellent sales history that help me land a nice contract for you."

"Hey," Rachel said, laughing, "just show me the money, Baby. Nepotism rules!"

The funny thing is, now that my sister is a new rising star, it will probably be ME hanging on to HER coattails. But alas, I tell her solemnly, with a reverent hand placed over my heart (and my tongue pressed firmly in cheek), "My sister must increase, and I must decrease."

Oh, well, it doesn't matter a bit whose star rises or sinks or stabilizes. At this stage of our lives, we're much more about sibling revelry than sibling rivalry.

And you can take that to the bank! (Right along with my sister's nicer advance check.)

Theriously.

○ ○ ○

The LORD bless you and keep you;
the LORD make His face shine upon
you and be gracious to you.

NUMBERS 6:24-25

18

Sentimental Journeys

We laugh, we cry, we make time fly.
Best friends are we, my sister and me.

Coffee with rich cream. Turn-of-the-century décor. Linen tablecloth, crystal, silver. Morning sunshine pours through the dining room's Victorian stained-glass window and spotlights the snowcapped mountains in the distance. On the table in front of me lies a Belgian waffle dripping with butter and orange marmalade, along with a local newspaper, a pen, and a journal. Nearby a waiter stands eager to keep my coffee warm and my breakfasting pleasant. I will spend the afternoon visiting and shopping among the interesting, laid-back people of Durango (or "Durangotangs" as the locals call themselves).

The strains of Pachelbel's Canon are drifting and swelling from somewhere above and behind my head. Let the ski buffs enjoy their fresh powder on the slopes today, for I'm enjoying my own personal Rocky Mountain high inside the classic old Strator Hotel Restaurant, enveloped by this beautiful piece of music. Involuntarily tears spring and fall as quickly as I wipe them from my cheek. (This happens to me in church, as well, when beautiful hymns are sung. I have some sort of musical-tear duct connection disorder. Patriotic songs can also do me in. I once tear-soaked a piece of pizza, sitting at a table with a bunch of kids at Chuck E. Cheese, when the robotic gorilla sang a very moving rendition of "I'm Proud to Be an American.")

Pachelbel's Canon (or "Taco Bell's Canon" as my kids call it), is a guaranteed, surefire tear trigger for me, transporting me to a memory so dear that I can almost feel myself standing in a small chapel near the back of a gorgeous sanctuary helping my little sister arrange her wedding train. Our mom, the other bridesmaids, and I are laughing and chatting when suddenly the bride takes hold of her train—and the proverbial reins. Putting her finger to her mouth she whispers, "Shhhh." Then quietly, her dark curls glistening against ivory satin, black eyes shining, Rachel says, "Listen, it's my wedding music. I want to absorb everything about this moment right now." We freeze and look like a posed arrangement of wedding dolls as the music of Pachelbel carves this moment into our collective memories.

"More coffee?" The waiter's question startles me back into the present.

'Yes, please, with cream and sugar." Sipping at the china rim, I pause to sigh and realize this is not the first time I've felt transported—caught in a time tunnel—by this particular piece of music.

A few years after the day I watched my sister go from a very simple Rachel Ann Arnold to the ultra-elegant Mrs. Rachel

Scott St. John-Gilbert III (I know, I also think it's a bit much), I purchased a tape of classical music, pushed it into my car stereo, and set out on my daily drive to pick up my then-school-aged children. Pachelbel's Canon began to play, and in a few minutes I was no longer in my rattletrap station wagon for "I'd gone to Carolina in my mind." Well, actually it was Virginia. I imagined myself back in that stained-glass church watching my beautiful sister float out of the dressing room on a cloud of satin and lace to the strains of this lovely piece of music, and then glide down the aisle toward her handsome groom. I could barely see the road; the sentimental tears were flowing so fast and so free.

When the song ended I looked up with a start and found I was in an unfamiliar town—I'd missed the exit to my children's school by more than 10 miles. The children looked bewildered when, 30 minutes late to pick them up, I explained, "I'm sorry. You see, I was at your Aunt Rachel's wedding five years ago."

Shortly after the "missed exit" experience, I visited my sister at her home in Virginia. One afternoon we went shopping at a mall and wandered together into a music store. Suddenly the familiar strains of Pachelbel began playing over the sound system.

"Rachel," I whispered loudly, "listen!"

"Oh, yes," she answered, a smile of remembrance spreading across her face, her dimples deepening. "It's my wedding song."

"I know, I know! Oh, Rachel, did I write you about the time I started listening to this piece in my station wagon when I was supposed to pick up the kids? I got so carried away with the music that the next thing I knew I'd missed..."

"Becky, are you crying?"

"Oh, I know (sniff) you just have to ignore me. I do this.

Wait a minute. I'm okay (pause, sniff). No, never mind, I'm losing it again."

"Becky, it's okay. Settle down. Remember, you were going to tell me what happened in your station wagon?"

"Oh, yes. Well, I was listening to this Canon."

"In D."

"Right. Is this not the most beautiful music you've ever heard? Oh, dear. I don't think I can finish the story. I'm getting choked up again. Do you have a tissue?"

At this point, a nearby group of milling people were beginning to stop and stare. Through my watery eyes and sniffs I looked at Rachel and then at the small crowd around us. I laughed and using my best Jewish-mother accent said, "I'll be all right. Just tawlk amongst yuhselves for a moment while I pull myself togethuh."

I never did manage to finish the tale verbally. (I had to write her the "Rest of the Story" later, when I could type and cry at the same time.) Rachel gave up on waiting for my tears to ebb and decided it would be more prudent to simply move me on down the mall toward The Sharper Image and Dillard's, significantly less emotional territory than the music store. I noticed she was also careful to steer me away from Things Remembered and Hallmark Sentimentals.

Though my sister adores classical music and usually has it playing in her home to calm any savage little beasties about, she doesn't share my tendency to weep uncontrollably when music touches her…and particularly not in public places. (Although she tells me when she's going through PMS, even the dreaded Barney songs can get her boo-hooing.)

I was relieved one Sunday morning to discover I wasn't completely alone in this musical-tears phenomenon. We were standing as a congregation singing the hymn "And Can It Be" when suddenly I made the mistake of really listening to the words. They were gorgeous, full of metaphor and meaning. "For O, my God, (mercy) found out me...My chains fell off, my heart was free." The hymnwriter (Charles Wesley) painted a word picture so intense that as the music pounded majestically from the organ and piano and congregation, the response of my heart to such an incredible gift increased. And, of course, the floodgates opened. "Amazing love! How can it be? That thou, My God, shouldst die for me?"

A woman behind me—a fellow book/music lover—understood my predicament. She tapped me on the shoulder, sacrificially split her Kleenex with me, then sniffed and mumbled, "Good writing, isn't it?"

There are sisters, like mine, who are there for you, your whole life through. And sometimes there are sisters of soul, with whom you bond for perhaps just a few seconds, but you are keenly aware that something special has passed between you, and you feel warmed, understood, and a little less alone in the world.

He will take great delight in you, he
will quiet you with his love, he will
rejoice over you with singing.

ZEPHANIAH 3:17 NIV

19

Wordy Women

*"Talking is the first voice of a writer. ....I write
the voices you hear every day—it's just that
people don't recognize how wonderfully
people talk. I think every time a person tells the
truth, that person is speaking beautifully."*

GRACE PALEY
QUOTED IN *Oprah Magazine*, July 26, 2006

My cell phone rang and it was my sister. I wanted to answer it
but I checked my watch and realized that my husband and I had
less than two minutes to get out of the house or we'd be late for
an appointment. "It's my sister, Rachel," I told Greg. "You want
to time how long it takes from the ring to the 'bing' showing that
her message is finished?"

He shook his head and laughed. "I never met women who
could talk so much and so long—even if no one is listening on
the other end of the phone."

"Do you mind it?" I asked.

"No, Babe," he said, grabbing his coat and heading for the car, "I'm just sort of fascinated by it. As long as you two don't expect me to be as wordy as you are, I'm happy to hear you talking. I think it's kind of cute."

Greg and I had all but forgotten Rachel's original ringy-dingy when, about a mile down the road my cell phone "binged"—indicating that Rachel had finished leaving her message and it was now ready for retrieval.

"Four minutes," I said.

"What?" Greg asked.

"It was a four-minute message. It's been four minutes since the phone ring and the message bing."

"That's nearly all your cell phone will hold."

"Yes, but it takes a lot of words for us to describe one day. Or one really good latte for that matter."

"Listen to the message, then tell me what she said," Greg said, looking at me curiously, as if I sprang from a family of verbose aliens.

I dialed up the answering service and six minutes later, gave Greg the abbreviated version of Rachel's recent trip to the Windy City. "She said Chicago was amazing. The parks were pristine, the hotel was exquisite, and the architecture fascinating and stunning."

"And this took four minutes?"

"Well, she used a lot more adjectives. She's really 'amazingly, pristinely, exquisitely, fascinating, and stunningly magnificent' at adjectives."

I called my sister back as soon as I had time to "adjectate" and pontificate, which is our family's specialty. I grew up shielded from knowing the definition of a "pregnant pause." All our pauses gave birth immediately…to lots and lots and lots of words. Silence is not golden in our family of origin. Where two or more are gathered together, it sounds like a meeting of excited barnyard hens.

But I digress. Back to my sister. I returned her call and then, chuckling, told her how amazed her brother-in-law was at the length of her phone messages. Twenty minutes later we had finished dissecting, evaluating, and examining three minutes worth of information.

Two days later she called again, only this time I was outside in my pristine garden, having missed the call altogether. When I dialed to retrieve the message, there was her peppy voice saying, "Hey, Beck! It's me! I was going to leave you a really short message because…well, I don't know why I was going to do that. I think it was because the last time we spoke I realized that Greg doesn't think I can just leave a brief message and the problem is…well, okay. I can't." A four-minute soliloquy later, I believed her.

Yesterday, a package arrived for Greg from my sister. "What do you think it is?" he asked.

"Maybe your birthday present?"

He opened it and smiled, "Yes, it is my birthday present!" Out of the mailing box, along with a wrapped gift, floated not one, not two, but *three* greeting cards. All for him! He held them up and looked at me quizzically.

"Well, Honey," I replied, "in our family, sometimes one card just can't say it all. Sometimes it takes two…or three."

Sometimes, there simply aren't enough words to convey—um, just about anything. Especially in our literary-loaded branch of the family tree. "Writers and Talkers R Us."

But might I add this bit of information to balance out our

heavily worded branches. We are also fabulous listeners and question-askers. There's a lovely equal-handed volleying to our typical family conversations. Should there be the beginning of a lull or the perception that someone might be pausing for intake of breath, we don't simply fill in the approaching silence with nonsensical chitchat. We ask good questions. Then we wait patiently, using active listening techniques, for the answer. If the answer is of the slightest interest ("yes" or "no" will do)—we'll follow up with even deeper and more insightful questions.

Though you may have wanted nothing more than to read the paper, drink your morning coffee, and stare into space, before you realize it any female member of our family tree—worth her weight in words—will have lassoed and hog-tied you into a meaningful conversation…that may never, ever end.

There was a fun nonsense song I used to sing to my first-graders when I taught school (before retiring after nine months of faithful service). It went something like, "This is the song that never ends. It just goes on and on my friend. Somebody started singing it, not knowing what it was, and now they keep on singing it forever just because…it is the song that never ends, it just goes on and on…" and so on.

For all eternity.

This is a pretty good picture of our family's conversations. Sure they may appear to end so we can sleep, or go back to our respective homes, or earn an income. But mark my many words, three days or three months later, one of us will call the other and say, "Now, you were discussing the latest Anne Lamott book…" or "Weren't you telling me about Trev's interest in theater?" And the bridge between the last conversation, however far removed, closes the gap and the eternal fire of communication continues.

For my sister and I, this is a good definition of heaven. For as Anne Morrow Lindbergh observed, "Good communication is as stimulating as black coffee, and just as hard to sleep after."

Our mother recently told us, however, that apparently not everyone feels the same way we women do about not taking time-outs between stimulating dialogue.

"I was talking to your father the other day on a long car trip, just chatting it up and having a ball when I paused to ask him, 'Don't you just love chitchat'?"

To which he replied, "Ruthie, Darling. I love to hear you talk, I do. But there's a difference between charming chitchat...and drivel."

Sad, but probably true.

Probably the biggest and perhaps the only major adjustment for me in my new marriage was to get used to the larger amounts of silence between sharing. Though Greg is one of the best conversationalists I know, he also enjoys television. He grew up with it as a comforting presence as a boy in his family of origin. Watching sports or the history channel (his favorites) allows him the luxury of turning off his mind while he rests from a long day of business communication (with talkative, verbose, creative types. He's a literary agent. Bless him).

He and his grown sons enjoy talking in more measured doses, but also like their silences and their TV sports. However, they do have "talking spurts" now and then, and if I catch them at just the right moment, I can rope them into a good conversation without their realizing it. But timing is everything. One of my most recent victories was when my stepson Troy came over and there was a big NBA play-off game on TV. However, he'd happened to mention, with active interest, a book he was reading and—*aha!*—I'd read it too. With a few well-placed questions, he was actually off the couch and…lo and behold, following me, chatting as I loaded the dishwasher.

"Wow," he said at one point.

"What?" I asked.

"I'm enjoying talking with you in the kitchen more than I was enjoying the NBA game."

I just smiled and savored the magic moment.

Then I called my sister and left a four-minute message about it.

○ ○ ○

Call to me, and I will answer you,
and show you great and mighty
things, which you do not know.

JEREMIAH 33:3 NKJV

20

The Greatest Gift a Sister Could Give

*"How do people make it through
life without a sister?"*

SARA CORPENING

My dear friend Melissa was like a sister to me during the years we lived next door to each other in Texas. She was a "spiritual sister," if you will. Though she's resigned to the fact that she can't fix every hurt or right every wrong in the world, her desire to help the underdog remains strong and is a part of who she will always be. If you happen to be low dog on the canine pole, this trait is a godsend.

Though I'd known Melissa for about two years at this point and we were close friends, one day in a casual conversation with her husband, Michael, he told me quite a story about Melissa and a little girl, a desperately sick child named Lynsey. "It happened about seven years ago, and Melissa doesn't talk about it because she doesn't want to call attention to herself. But, Becky, it's a beautiful story. Ask her about it."

"So fill me in on what happened," I asked Melissa one day as we sat on the back porch overlooking the lake where we lived, our legs propped up to catch a few rays (our motto being "tanned fat looks better than white fat").

"Well," began Melissa, "for a long time I didn't want to tell this to many people, but I think it may be time. I didn't want to draw attention to myself, but I'm realizing there may be a greater good that can come from sharing what happened."

She shifted to get more comfortable in her chair and took a sip of iced coffee before diving into the tale.

"When Michael and I were in Austin, we lived next door to a young couple named Becky and Ed."

"Becky?"

"I know, it seems like my best next-door friends all turn out to be named Becky. Anyway, their son Jordan and my Josh became fast friends. They were almost inseparable." Melissa went on to explain that after many years of waiting and praying, God granted Ed and Becky a second child, a little girl whom they named Lynsey.

"When Lynsey was about 13 months old, Becky noticed her daughter's eyes looked awfully puffy. The next day Becky took Lynsey to the pediatrician, expecting to be told she was an overcautious mom. But after what seemed like hours, the doctor returned with the report, 'For some unknown reason,' he said, 'Lynsey appears to be spilling protein into her urine.'

"The next day, they sent Lynsey for some medical tests and

eventually discovered she had Nephrotic Syndrome, which is caused by a rare disease called Focal Segmental Glomerular Sclerosis. Sadly, we got lots of practice pronouncing this tongue twister, because short of a kidney transplant—there is no cure.

"The doctors assured Ed and Becky this was a slow-moving disease. Through medication Lynsey might be able to keep her own kidneys for up to five years.

"Then, just nine months later, a biopsy showed the disease had spread much more rapidly than any of them expected. Lynsey's kidneys were functioning at 15 percent of a normal organ."

Melissa sighed and shook her head recalling how fast Lynsey went downhill and how desperate Becky began to feel. "Lynsey dropped off the bottom of the growth cart. By the time she was two her entire body was puffed up, filled with toxins her kidneys could no longer filter. The doctors said it was time to consider a transplant. Of course Ed and Becky were tested, but for medical reasons they were unable to be donors."

Curious, I asked, "Melissa, how could a tiny child receive an adult-sized kidney anyway?"

"You know, that's really interesting. An adult can donate a kidney to a child, and the kidney will actually shrink to fit. The donor's remaining kidney will also swell to accommodate the lost organ."

"Amazing. Go on."

"About that time our family moved from Austin to Houston, but my friendship with Becky was by this time more like sisterhood. Maybe because I grew up with only brothers and no sisters, God's given me two Becky-sisters to love and enjoy! So Becky called one day and told me Lynsey's blood type was O-negative. I drew in a long breath. This was my blood type. After I hung up I told Michael and the kids I wanted to be tested as a possible donor for Lynsey."

"How did they react?"

"There was some concern among family and friends, but Michael and I were in agreement. All we had to do was glance at our two healthy kids and know how we'd feel if one of them were in Lynsey's condition. My sister-friend's child was dying—and I had an opportunity to possibly help her live, with minimal risk to my long-term health. How could I say no?"

"Melissa, lots of people would."

"I would never have been able to live with myself if I didn't at least try. So I drove to Galveston to be tested."

"Annnnnddd?"

"And...the news was great. Lynsey and I were a match!"

I smiled and leaned forward, "Oh my goodness. I bet Becky was delirious with happiness."

"Oh she was, she was." Melissa's voice broke just a bit with the emotion of the memory. "She cried with relief and gratitude, but our joy was short-lived. After some further testing, the coordinator canceled the transplant. As it turned out, due to her deteriorating condition requiring blood transfusions, the puzzle pieces of our blood cells would no longer line up well enough to risk the transplant."

"They must have been devastated."

"We all were. It was horrible. I'll never forget the day we received the news that we couldn't proceed. We were sitting in the playroom of the children's hospital, sitting around a child-sized table in pint-sized chairs. Me, Ed, Becky, Lynsey's grandparents, and the surgeon. Becky is a fighter. She cried and begged the surgeon to please think of some other way to save her baby. The surgeon finally broke down and cried too, saying, 'Becky if there was any way I could you know that I would.' "

At this point, Melissa brushed away a tear. "All of us grownups sitting in these tiny chairs, helpless as small children to change Lynsey's fate. It was almost unbearably sad."

By this time a lump formed in my own throat and I swallowed hard, waiting for Melissa to gather her thoughts and continue the story.

"After that Lynsey had to go back on dialysis, but we all knew it was a temporary measure holding off the inevitable. Then one day, a few months later I was vacuuming at home and received a call from the transplant coordinator at UTMC."

"Yes?"

"She said, 'Melissa, there's a new machine at the University of Alabama—only one of its kind—and it has the ability to go deeper into the makeup of the blood cells. There's a slight chance that with this new technology, we might be able to help yours and Lynsey's blood match after all.' "

"What an emotional rollercoaster!"

Melissa nodded. "You're not kidding. My first thought was 'Can any of us take this again? The buildup of hope? The potential for more devastation?' We'd just about come to peace with the last round of bad news. But I had no choice; I knew we had to try. Two days later I returned home from grocery shopping, and Michael met me at the door, his eyes wide. He said only three words, 'It's on, Melissa'—before I collapsed into his arms with relief, followed by panic. We had so much to get together and only 24 hours before the operation was scheduled to take place.

"We scrambled for airplane tickets, cancelled meetings, got family to keep our kids…"

I laughed and said, "I can just hear you, Melissa. 'I'm sorry I won't be at the PTO bake sale, I'll be in the hospital donating a kidney next week."

Melissa grinned. "Actually, I was surprisingly calm during all of the trauma."

"And so?"

"And so there were a few more scares, a period of time when we thought Lynsey might be rejecting my kidney, but the long and short of it is that the operation was a 100 percent success.

"Within the next year, Becky and I were sitting in her living room laughing and talking when suddenly we saw my daughter Sarah's head peek up over the kitchen counter. Sarah was about five years old at the time. The next thing we knew, Lynsey's tiny four-year-old head appeared, grabbing hold of Sarah's suspenders and pulling her down to the floor in a wrestling match. That was one skirmish between kids we were delighted to witness."

"What an amazing story!" I exclaimed. "Melissa, I'd really like to write about this. And with your permission, I'd like to talk to Becky and get a few comments from her.

"If you think our story might encourage other people to consider organ donation, sure."

A few days later I was on the phone with Becky. She was delighted I'd called.

"Not a day goes by that I don't think of Melissa," Becky said. "Every time I look at Lynsey I know she's alive because my friend's kidney is inside her body, working beautifully."

"Melissa said you and she were like sisters. I think that when your best friend shares an organ with your child, it definitely shoots you somewhere between friend and relative—maybe even above it."

"Isn't that the truth? It's like Melissa is always near my heart. Some part of me is saying a perpetual prayer of gratitude. I mean, how do you thank someone for giving you a healthy child? Lynsey is pitching for her softball team and driving all of us crazy at times, as only an active nine-year-old can. And we love her more than life itself."

In an anonymous letter to Ann Landers, Melissa summed up her feelings about the risks of live kidney donation:

> Since donating a kidney, my remaining kidney has functioned better than my two kidneys functioned before…I know of no cases in which a donor's health was compromised by giving a kidney.
>
> As to fear of death during or after surgery, the Bible says there is no greater love than to give your life for a friend. My faith allayed my fears. I had a feeling of absolute peace and certainty when I made this decision…
>
> Next to giving birth to my two children, donating my kidney was the most rewarding experience of my life.

How do you thank someone for saving your child's life? You cherish your child and her smiles all the days of her beautiful life.

That's all a soul sister like Melissa could ever ask or want in exchange.

○ ○ ○

There is a friend who sticks closer than a brother [or sister].

PROVERBS 18:24 NIV

Dear Friend

I hope this little book has been an experience of sisterhood for you. As you've allowed me this time to share sisterly stories and secrets, laughter and lessons, my prayer is that you will also feel you've met a sister of soul in the time we've shared. That you might feel warmed and a little less alone in the world.

Isn't that what sisters do for one another?

From Becky Freeman Johnson...

○ ○ ○

With my new marriage and a nearby (and ever-growing) passel of children-turned-adults, I've taken on lots of happy new roles: wife, mom, mother-in-law, stepmom, and grandmother. I also support my husband, Greg, in his literary business with editing, client support, and hostessing.

Because of these wonderful changes and the time it takes to be available to my family, I rarely do public speaking. However, if you need a good speaker for your event, may I recommend my good friends Gene and Carol Kent at Speak Up Speaker Services? They can be contacted at www.speakupspeakerservices.com.

For updates on my books and other news or information visit me at

www.yellowroseeditorial.com

Becky Freeman Johnson's brand-new series

HeartLite Stories

will bless your heart and tickle your funny bone!

BECKY'S TRADEMARK HUMOR AND WARMTH SHINE
IN HER HEARTLITE STORIES. EACH ATTRACTIVE, HARDCOVER BOOK
OVERFLOWS WITH STORIES OF JOY AND INSPIRATION.

It's Fun to Be Your Friend

When lives intersect and a bond between women is formed, the treasures of faithfulness, loyalty, and authenticity are discovered. Becky reflects on all these gifts and more as she shares joy-filled stories about how a cherished friend knows us better than we know ourselves, extends forgiveness and grace, believes in our goodness and gifts, offers silence or conversation when we need it, and becomes a reflection of unconditional love.

It's Fun to Be Your Sister

In this gathering of delightful stories about the connection between sisters and sisters-of-the-heart, each engaging chapter reveals why a sister is the gift that keeps on giving. Women with sisters are able to laugh more at life and at themselves, rest in what they have in common, find blessings and inspiration in each other, walk through life with joy and laughter, and share the biggest trials and the simplest pleasures.

It's Fun to Be a Mom

Becky invites women to take a break, catch their breath, and savor stories of pure joy about the privilege, the labor, and the gift of motherhood. These engaging, short tales lead moms to embrace the habits of highly real moms, the strange miracle of breast feeding, the loss of brain cells when one gains a child, the quest for sleep and romance after kids, and the amazing strength of their own mothers.

It's Fun to Be a Grandma

A grandma is to be revered and celebrated. And Becky does just that with stories from her life as a granddaughter and grandmother. With warmth, insight, and her trademark humor, Becky lifts up these special women who believe wholeheartedly in their children and grandchildren, become the keeper of stories and memories, have incomparable strength of spirit and heart, show the women following them how to live richly, and never tire of talking to or about their grandbabies.